I like to rise when the sun she rises
Early in the morning,
I like to hear them small birds singing
Merrily upon the laylum.
And hurrah for the life of a country boy
And to ramble in the new-mown hay.

'Country Life', *chorus*

# Singing
## *like* Larks

*A Celebration of Birds
in Folk Songs*

*Andrew* **Millham**

*Saraband*

Published by Saraband
3 Clairmont Gardens,
Glasgow, G3 7LW, UK

www.saraband.net

ISBN: 9781913393663

*Every effort has been made by the author to check the copyright status
of the verses in this book and to obtain permission to print any verses
that may be subject to copyright. The majority are traditional songs
that are no longer in copyright, most of them listed in the Roud Folk
Song Index. Others have been included here by express permission of
the copyright owner, including songs by the Copper family and Ashley
Hutchings, for which grateful thanks are acknowledged.*

Printed and bound in Great Britain by Clays Ltd, Elcograf S.p.A.

1  2  3  4  5  6  7  8  9  10

# Contents

# Foreword

Two years or so ago, during the second Covid lockdown, I received an email from a young man. He asked my advice on his idea for a book, which at that time he had titled *Birds and the Folk Song Tradition.*

As a published author, I'm often approached by new writers with an idea for a book they want to write. But in many cases, they either lack the genuine expertise to write about their chosen subject, or they come to me with the germ of an idea, which will need more research and development before it can be submitted to a publisher.

But the book proposal Andrew Millham sent to me was not just a really good idea. It also had answers to the three key questions I always suggest my MA Nature and Travel Writing students at Bath Spa University ask themselves: "Why This? Why Now? Why Me?"

Despite his youth – Andrew is still only in his early twenties – he had come up with an idea for a book that covered a fascinating and neglected subject, the importance of birds in folk song – Why This? It is also very topical – Why Now? And crucially, Andrew had the knowledge, expertise and enthusiasm to write this book, having already published several magazine articles both about birds and about folk song – Why Me?

Less than a year earlier, during the first lockdown, I had published my lockdown diary, *Skylarks with Rosie*, with the wonderful Sara Hunt at Saraband. Having worked closely with Sara and her team, I knew they would be the perfect publisher for Andrew's book; they may be a small outfit, but they punch well above their weight, and are highly respected in the world of publishing.

The rest, as the cliché goes, is history. Andrew's book, now retitled *Singing Like Larks,* is here in front of me. And what a beautiful, informative and fascinating book it is! I love the way the format mimics a record album, with each of the dozen 'tracks' (chapters) based on a bird: starting with the Nightingale, followed by the Wren, Skylark, Robin, Turtle Dove, Cuckoo, domestic Chicken, Magpie, Blackbird, Owl, and Hawk, before ending with the Swan. In each chapter he seamlessly blends the behaviour of the bird with its place in the history of folk song, all written in a lively and engaging style.

What also comes across so strongly in Andrew's writing is his passion for the subject. When we first spoke, he told me that "This is an opportunity to write about what I love." He has certainly done that, and, as he reminds us in the book's Introduction, this is what we love, too:

> *We are the "folk" in "folk song" – the songs belong to us all.*
> *They **are** us.*

So, I am delighted, proud and honoured to write this Foreword, to a book which I hope will help you understand the deep and complex relationship between birds and folk music, remind you about things you know – and tell you things you didn't – and most of all, make you listen afresh to both music and bird song, those wonders of the human and the natural world.

STEPHEN MOSS
Author and naturalist
Mark, Somerset

# Introduction

## The Birds in the Spring

SNOW CAME AS A SURPRISE. It was mid-March, and spring had sprung down south. Malham Tarn – being so high up – was yet to follow. Hills were white and puddles frozen. I was visiting for an environmental science field trip, one month after my twentieth birthday. Throughout the week, waves of ever-worsening news headlines lit up my phone screen whenever there was a flicker of signal: 'Coronavirus: A National Emergency', 'Mass Gatherings to be Banned', 'Lockdown Britain'. Separate from the chaos, in a faraway bubble close to the Yorkshire clouds, our small group felt like the last people on Earth.

Before breakfast each morning, I strolled downhill to a bird hide on the edge of the tarn and listened to the water lapping, interrupted only by the honking of Canada geese. Elsewhere, schools were closing, flights grounding and my fellow fieldtrippers from abroad were frantically making alternative travel arrangements for the end of the week. When I returned to the imposing Georgian field studies centre on the final morning, the lead tutor stood at the head of the group and delivered a dramatic speech: "We're going back into a different world to the one we left." He was right and, for me, in more ways than one.

My dad pulled into the gravel car park, and I emerged through the hefty black door of the field centre with my burgundy coloured holdall cutting into my right shoulder. Car loaded up; one last stroll down to the tarn's edge; time to go. Once we hit the motorway, southbound, I flicked on the radio for a bit of background noise and the little text bar floating across the screen read: *Mark Radcliffe's BBC2 Folk Show.* Basking in gentle quietness after a week of room-sharing, I stared out with my head vibrating against the window, watching the cat's eyes fling past. Then I heard it: four thick Sussex accents singing about nature, unaccompanied, in gloriously unpolished harmony. It sounded ancient, honest, familiar and straight from the soil. I was instantly hooked.

Those voices were the Copper Family of Rottingdean, a Sussex farming folk dynasty with an unbroken singing tradition stretching back at least 300 years.

I remembered that name – Copper – for the whole ride home and looked them up as soon as I got in. A love of traditional music gripped hold of me. Hours of listening to the Coppers (whom we will meet again in Chapter One) led me from one song to another, one singer to another, and it was not long before I noticed a theme running through the genre, popping up in old lyrics time and time again – birds.

Birds surround us. Low and high; land and sky; pylon and pavement; mountain and moor. They soundtrack our lives with their rattling, chirruping, whistling songs, and feature in so many of our own. We are often compelled to sing about what we love, and folk songs showcase just what birds mean to us – even if we sometimes forget.

We are the "folk" in "folk song" – the songs belong to us all. They *are* us. They chronicle the history of people and places, and we are incredibly fortunate to inherit a vast stock of timeless lyrics and melodies from our ancestors. Whilst we are here, our role is to cherish them, learn from them, put our own creative spin on them, and deliver them on to their next custodians. And yet, the unfortunate truth is that this living musical tradition is dwindling – in danger of disappearing, even.

Ornithological folk songs are a threatened species – out of place in today's fast-paced technological world. The majority of traditional songs are no longer passed on, very rarely sung and instead buried in the yellowing pages of dusty ballad books in silent libraries. The people that created and learnt these songs looked to the skies, to themselves and to one another for entertainment – no smartphones, no PlayStations. Birds were a major part of life. Rising early and retiring late, these people's days were serenaded with birdsong, and so they sang about it. Today, our lives are seemingly too busy to watch the birds, our days too jam-packed to sing a 'boring' old song. Never have we been more connected with each other, yet so disconnected from nature and wildlife.

*Singing Like Larks*, therefore, serves as a treasure trove of bird-filled folk songs, and an unadulterated celebration of our musicality. To rediscover a love for these songs, many lost somewhere along the way, is to rediscover our shared love for the birds themselves. My hope is for you, the reader, to lift the lyrics from these pages; sing them, share them, bring them back to life and let them soar again. You'll find a list of links to where you can hear versions of these songs if you scan the QR code printed on the last page of this book.

Within this book you will not only encounter songs, but also the coastal and country characters who once sang them, and those who sing them still. After spending countless hours with singers like Bob Roberts, Harry Cox and Sarah Makem on the page, they feel to me like old friends. I cannot wait for you to meet them. A first-hand knowledge, appreciation and respect for wildlife is reflected wholeheartedly in their songs.

From a fiery waxwing in frosty January feeding from a rowan tree, a swallow in May diving for an aquatic invertebrate lunch, a fledged house sparrow in July nibbling at a garden bird feeder, to a robin burnished by the flagging October sun. Let us take a moment, like those before us, to raise our voices for the cycling seasons, and the birds that follow them.

Before we venture any further, I should note that this is by no means a comprehensive collection of bird-related folk songs. Rather, it is a curated selection and an account of my wild journey into the world of traditional folk music so far. This is a genre with countless nooks (or should I say 'rooks') and crannies: always a new singer, always a new song. I am certain that, in time, I will discover songs with ornithological lyrics that may have been better placed in a chapter, but this is the inevitable, delightful reality of folk music: like a foraging robin, rustling around for wormy goodness – the further you dig, the more you uncover. With that in mind I attempt this book.

Birds and folk songs share something in common. Both have the ability to open our eyes to the endless wonder flying just beyond our doorsteps. All we have to do is look … and listen.

It has been a good while since that long drive home from Malham Tarn, but I will never forget the feeling those old voices stirred in me, nor the ancient song they were singing: 'The Birds in the Spring'.

## The Birds in the Spring

One May morning early I chanced for to roam,
And strolled through the field by the side of the grove.
It was there I did hear the harmless birds sing,
And you never heard so sweet, and you never heard so sweet,
You never heard so sweet as the birds in the spring.

At the end of the grove I sat myself down
And the song of the nightingale echoed all round,
Their song was so charming, their notes were so clear,
No music, no songster, no music, no songster,
No music, no songster can with them compare.

All you that come here the small birds to hear,
I'll have you pay attention so pray all draw near.
And when you are growing old you will have this to say,
That you never heard so sweet, you never heard so sweet,
You never heard so sweet as the birds on the spray!

# Sweet Nightingale

## *Luscinia megarhynchos*

*They went arm in arm along the road 'til they came to a stream,*
*And they both sat down together, love, to hear the nightingale sing.*
                                        – 'The Bold Grenadier'

THE BEST SINGERS are not always who we expect them to be.

Framed by golden fields, lively conversation spills out of the village pub and into the evening silence: stories, jokes, raucous laughter and intense debate about the weather – which is never small talk for a farmer. Sooted-up clay pipes lie on the counter, taken up one by one, and muddy hobnail boots rest by a glowing brick hearth.

A weathered man sits in the corner, glass in hand, blending into the scene. Wrinkled. Worn. Bent almost double from decades of working outdoors, brow as furrowed as the fields he once ploughed. He stands up slowly, sures himself with a wooden stick and clears his throat. A howl from behind the bar calls for a hush:

"The singer's on his feet!"

Through windows ajar, a nightingale's mellifluous trill sounds above the lull and, looking somewhere into the beamed ceiling, the man lets fly:

Green Bushes *(verses 1-3)*
As I was a-walking one morning in Spring
To hear the birds whistle and the nightingales sing
I met a young damsel and sweetly sang she,
"Down by the green bushes where he thinks to meet me."

"I'll buy you fine beavers and a fine silken gown
I'll buy you fine petticoats, flounced down to the ground
If you will prove loyal and constant to me;
Forsake your own true love and marry with thee."

"I want none of your beavers, nor none of your hose,
Do you think I'm so poor I would marry for clothes?
But if you'll prove constant and true unto me,
I'll forsake my own true love and marry with thee."

Right up until the close of the nineteenth century, such tender traditional songs as 'Green Bushes' were sung in common parlance by everyday countrymen and women in the fields, pubs and cottages of Britain and Ireland. Songs without known origin, passed down orally from parents and grandparents, telling all manner of tales spanning the full spectrum of human emotion and experience. Songs which describe historical figures and events, songs which bring folklore to life and songs which hold lifetimes of learned wisdom within their verses. Truly, traditional singing was a cornerstone of village culture and identity.

At first glance, nightingales too look as modest and humble as a farm labourer. Medium-sized and plain brown all over, wing feathers ribbed like a corduroy jacket, hiding themselves within impenetrable bush and thicket – similar in many ways to their fellow scrub-dwellers. But the moment they open their beaks, the world is alight with an unparalleled majesty of sound. It is clear that to truly know a bird – or a person, for that matter – you must first hear their voice.

According to folk songs, the nightingale sings, whilst other small birds merely whistle. Their fiery song has elevated them among their peers and led them to star disproportionately in our own lyrics. The Roud Folk Song Index, compiled by folklorist Steve Roud, is a database with around 25,000 records containing almost every folk song in the English language; if a snatch of lyrics has been scribbled down, printed, published or recorded (be that by the artist themselves or with a microphone by a song collector), then it is likely to be in there. The database hosts 570 songs with 'nightingale' in the title (admittedly referring sometimes to the name of a ship), second only to the blackbird with 611. 'Green Bushes' is included as Roud #1040.

In the song itself, the woman is content to steal away from under the 'green bushes' with another more rousing suitor. This seems harsh and reckless, but the manner of courtship is no different from that of the fiercely competitive nightingale. Unpaired males sing through the day to defend their territory and at night in a constant attempt to seduce a female – a behaviour which is preserved in their Old English name, "*nigtegale*", which translates to "night songster". Is this similarity between human and bird wooing intentionally highlighted in 'Green Bushes' by the inclusion of the nightingale? Maybe the nightingale is included as a poetic device to express the naturalistic depths of human desire in a less explicit, close-to-nature way. We can never know for sure.

I got caught up in a nightingale verbal dispute when I visited Fingringhoe Wick nature reserve, Essex, in May 2022. The site is a reclaimed gravel pit, described as a "lunar landscape" when purchased in 1961, and now contains a mixture of ecosystems. Woodland, meadow, scrubland, coastal mudflat and saltmarsh are all stitched together to form a mosaic of habitats. With between forty and forty-five individuals, the reserve hosts around one percent of the entire UK nightingale population and was the first location for folk singer and conservationist Sam Lee's inspiring "Singing with Nightingales" experience. Sam takes guests out in all weathers, where they wait for the sun to set and sing folk songs in harmony with the birds themselves.

My visit was in broad daylight, about a year after beginning this book, and I was joined by Essex Wildlife Trust ranger, Alex Long – a tall man in his mid-twenties. Crunching footsteps sounded our progress along a gravel track, and bright yellow gorse flowers fragranced the air with sweet coconut. Flowing discussion was severed as a burst of unpredictable song sounded directly above our heads from deep within a white-blooming hawthorn tree. The vocalist was completely invisible – for all we knew, it could have been the tree singing.

Within a few moments, another braggadocious male responded with even more sophisticated verbalisations, in an identical tree a few metres along the path. He would copy, then embellish. Alex described it as a "rap battle" of sorts – both

9

parties taking turns to try and outdo the other, like in 'Dueling Banjos'. With eleven to twelve hundred notes at the nightingale's disposal, it is a foreign language, but not one that can be learnt on Duolingo. Intoxicatingly precise warbles, gurgles and theatrical trills transformed the briar and bramble into a wild stage of whistling warfare. I don't know which nightingale emerged triumphant, but the battle was mightily fought.

> It is twelve long months since first we met
> So early in the spring
> When the small birds do whistle and
> The nightingales do sing. (x2)
>
> And if ever I return again
> I'll take that boy inside
> And I'll roll him in my very own arms
> Down by the tan yard side.

> – 'The Tan Yard Side', trad. English folk song.
> Sam Lee's recording has nightingale song in the background.

* * *

There is rarely a middle ground when it comes to the folkloric portrayal of the nightingale. It is either an extreme positive or negative, with little in between. Throughout history, from Homer's *Odyssey* and Ovid's *Metamorphoses* to T.S. Eliot's 'The Waste Land', the nightingale's song has been heard as a lament – the soundtrack of tragedy. Such despondency was directly challenged by poets during the Romantic era who perceived this bird to be an artist in its own right, a spokesperson for all wildlife broadcasting creativity, purity and virtue.

# Sweet Nightingale

Keats' 'Ode to a Nightingale' (1819) depicts the nightingale as a poetic genius, achieving heights of artistic spontaneity that we humans can only dream of:

> That thou, light-winged Dryad of the trees
> In some melodious plot
> Of beechen green, and shadows numberless,
> Singest of summer in full throated ease.

An impression of ethereal beauty is conjured by "Dryad", akin to a nymph or tree spirit, whilst "melodious plot" poses a double meaning. It seems at first to refer simply to a stand of beech trees alive with music, but figuratively hints at some sinister ulterior motive behind the birdsong, sensed by the morose speaker. Later on in the poem the nightingale is said to be "too happy in thine happiness", practically mocking him in his sorrow. Keats' nightingale is either a magical creature, fit to fly amongst fairies, or a laughing 'plotting' trickster. No middle ground.

The traditional folk song, 'Sweet Nightingale' (also known as 'Down in the Valleys Below') also highlights this 'either-or', positive-negative battleground of interpretations. The words brim with the joys of courtship when read aloud as a poem, but the slow, plaintive tune which is historically paired with these lyrics seems to tell a different story…

> Sweet Nightingale
> My sweet-heart, come along.
> Don't you hear the fond song
> The sweet notes of the nightingale flow?
> Don't you hear the fond tale,
> Of the sweet nightingale,
> As she sings in the valleys below?

# Singing Like Larks

Pretty Betty, don't fail,
For I'll carry your pail
Safe home to your cot as we go;
You shall hear the fond tale
Of the sweet nightingale,
As she sings in the valleys below.

Pray let me alone,
I have hands of my own,
Along with you Sir, I'll not go,
To hear the fond tale
Of the sweet nightingale,
As she sings in the valleys below.

Pray sit yourself down
With me on the ground,
On this bank where the primroses grow,
You shall hear the fond tale
Of the sweet nightingale,
As she sings in the valleys below.

The couple agreed,
And were married with speed,
And soon to the church they did go;
No more is she afraid
For to walk in the shade,
Nor sit in those valleys below.

– Trad, from Rev. Baring-Gould's Songs of the West (1905 edn.).

This song is sometimes referred to as the "Cornish Anthem" despite this species not being known to have nested in Cornwall within living memory. A version of these lyrics was first published in Robert Bell's *Poems of the Peasantry of England* (1857), with the accompanying note:

# Sweet Nightingale

*This curious ditty — said to be a translation from the ancient Cornish tongue… we first heard in Germany… The singers were four Cornish miners, who were at the time, 1854, employed at some lead mines near the town of Zell. The leader, or captain, John Stocker, said that the song was an established favourite with the lead miners of Cornwall and Devonshire, and was always sung on the pay-days and at the wakes; and that his grandfather, who died 30 years before at the age of a hundred years, used to sing the song, and say that it was very old.*

'Sweet Nightingale' is an example of a chorus song. Popular in the English tradition, these songs are usually led by one singer, with everyone else joining in for the repeated refrain – in this case, some variation of "Don't you hear the fond tale, / Of the sweet nightingale, / As she sings in the valleys below?"

In his own words, Anglican priest and folk song collector Rev. Sabine Baring-Gould (1834–1924) discovered the thoughtful tune from "a good many old men in Cornwall" who all sung it "to the same air". These old men asserted that this song is actually a duet, with each final line meant to be shared between two voices with one answering the other, like two male nightingales from within the hedgerow. Such a melancholic tune invites a certain eeriness and unsettling feeling that not all is as it seems. For me, I always imagine that the man in the song has grown old, lost his sweetheart, and is recalling his youth and the nightingale's song by singing. The intriguing tune is surely part of the reason why 'Sweet Nightingale' remains popular amongst folk singers today, ultimately spotlighting the nightingale in a beam of measured beauty.

Bucolic traditional songs like 'Charming Molly' – hailing from the fields and farms of Britain – avoid any notions of sadness or negativity, simply extolling the wonders of springtime beauty.

### Charming Molly

Charming Molly, fair, brisk and gay like nightingales
   in May
All round her eyelids young Cupids play,
She has eyes so bright they shine
Black as any berry, cheeks like any cherry.
Charming Molly with sparkling eyes.

See how the swain do admire and desire a pretty little girl,
To hold her hand it burns like sparkling fire,
In her face these things are seen,
Violets, roses, lilies and daffadown-dillies.
Charming Molly she is all divine.

Surely there's no one loves a pretty woman if she be not
   common-oh,
Surely such beauty most men admire,
Surely there's no one can them despise
Because they are so pretty and they talk so witty,
Charming Molly with sparkling eyes.

I first came across 'Charming Molly' in my dog-eared copy of Bob Copper's (1915-2004) award-winning debut book, *A Song for Every Season*, which recounts a farming year in his home of Rottingdean, East Sussex, and the old land workers and shepherds known to him. Bob was an out-and-out countryman with dark, slightly curled hair, light humour and a healthy disrespect for authority.

As a boy, the elderly folks in the village – born in the first half of the nineteenth century – were well-versed in farming methods unchanged since Saxon times. In their younger days they had ploughed land with teams of oxen, sowed seeds by hand, reaped corn with sickles and threshed out the grain with flails. Their lives moved at a slower pace but were extremely full. Slowly, one by one, a young Bob saw this older generation thin out and pass on, taking many ancient songs to the grave when they died. Fewer and fewer youngsters were interested in learning them, and over time an ever-decreasing number of people were able or willing to sing old songs. This filled Bob from an early age with a determination to save as many as he could – especially his own family's collection of songs (but we'll talk about those in a moment).

In *A Song for Every Season*, Bob describes Rottingdean as lying "twixt downs and sea" in the lap of the South Downs. Until around the mid-twentieth century it was chiefly a farming community, with a touch of longshoreman work. Locals took pride in their working relationship with the natural world, and often sung about it. Village life was hard but uncomplicated, and a man could live and die without stepping five miles away from the town in which he was born. Countryside settlements were like islands, intruded upon only by pedlars and itinerant workers, and each inhabitant was vibrantly individual, their dress and manner of speaking uninfluenced by outside forces. They were unashamedly themselves.

Bob's grandfather, James Copper (1845–1924), was affectionately dubbed "Brasser". He was a broad-shouldered man, bold and stately, with a booming voice. As a shepherd boy from the age of nine, he watched over the old hills and kept the sheep off the growing crops, and in later years became farm foreman. Singing was his favourite pastime, and Brasser maintained into old age that "Any dam' fool can sing at night. That takes a good man to sing a song afore brakfus." One of Bob's earliest memories is of his grandfather singing one morning:

> I remember as a small boy of about five lying on a heap of straw on the granary floor watching Grand-dad mend holes in an old cornsack draped across his knee with a curved packing needle threaded with twine that smelt like turpentine. I lay there watching and listening intently as the ancient story unfolded, for the old man was singing, in a deep, resonant bass, a song he had heard from his own grandfather when he had been my age.[1]

This was not any old song; it was a Copper song. Singing runs in the Copper family, and they have been the loving custodians of around sixty traditional songs for centuries – including 'Charming Molly'. The family was once connected with farming and shepherding, and the collection they have amassed includes many Sussex shepherding songs (around 250,000 sheep grazed the chalky downland turf between Beachy Head and Steyning in the nineteenth century), plough songs and ancient ballads that modern-day Coppers still sing. British folk songs are usually sung in solo, unaccompanied verse, but the Coppers sing in rich two-part harmonies – like hymns in worship of their native land. In every sense, they enjoy "'armony in the 'ome".

The parish records of St Margaret's Church in the heart of Rottingdean detail the marriage of an Edward Coper in 1593. Bob jokes in his book that over the 400 years since, his family at least acquired another "p" to their name, "if little else". A quiet, green-canopied spot in the graveyard hosts a gathering of weathered headstones, decorated with luminous lichen and all engraved with the same surname, the older ones smoothed and barely legible. Lovingly named "Coppers' Corner" by locals, their long station in this part of Sussex is literally set in stone.

As members of the family departed from this life, the family songs may too have been buried in "Coppers' Corner" alongside them. The following turn of events prevented that from happening, as if the title of one of their songs called out, 'Come Write Me Down', and a Mrs Kate Lee dutifully obliged.

Come write me down, ye powers above,
The man that first created love...

In 1897, Kate Lee came to Rottingdean from London. She was a folk song collector and had heard about the singing of two rough and ready brothers – Brasser and Tommy Copper – down in The Black Horse, the local sixteenth-century white-washed pub on the High Street. Wishing to know more, she invited them up to the "big house" in the village where a grand politician called Sir Edward Carson lived – quite a change from the dusty tap room. They donned their Sunday best and attended. A full bottle of whisky, two cut-glass tumblers and a decanter of water greeted them on the table, which defrosted any stiffness induced by singing in such a formal setting.

Mrs Lee feverishly scribbled down words and music as the men oscillated between singing and drinking – sharing songs of land and sea, and those men and women who, over the centuries, have struggled to lift a living from them. Neither party left until the bottle of whisky was empty, and the notebook on

# Singing Like Larks

Mrs Lee's lap was brimming. Several meetings followed, and Kate returned to London with a "copper-ful of songs" (as it was later referred to), using her findings to form the Folk Song Society – existing today as the English Folk Dance and Song Society. Both brothers were made honorary members, and of them she wrote:

> *They were so proud of their Sussex songs and sang with an enthusiasm grand to hear and when I questioned them as to how many they thought they could sing, they said they thought about 'half a hundred'. You only had to start either of them on the subject of a song and they would commence at once. 'O, Mr. Copper, can you sing me a love song, a sea song or a plough song?' It did not matter what it was, they looked at each other significantly, and with perfectly grave faces off they would go. Mr. Thomas Copper's voice was as flexible as a bird's.[2]*

Sometime later, in 1936, Brasser's second son, Jim Copper (Bob's quick-witted father, also farm bailiff in his time) wrote out the words to around sixty of the family songs, forming a songbook which he hoped would live on after him. Jim opened the collection by penning a rhyme in the flyleaf, which begins:

Here we have a little book,
If through its pages you will look,
You'll find the songs you ought to know,
So have some beer and let her go.

Soon, Bob and his cousin Ron were the young men in the family and one day they got together, shook hands and vowed not to be "weak links in the chain". They sang together and with their parents whenever possible – at home, in The Black Horse and they were even invited to sing at The Royal Albert Hall in 1952 (but that is another story entirely!). To Bob's delight, his children – John and Jill – also inherited a love of the family songs, and today three generations of Coppers continue to sing from Jim's old songbook. Many of their songs preserve a love of birds and in the lyrics, unlike in real life, the nightingale is jubilantly visible to all.

> I wish I was a butterfly, I would fly to my love's breast,
> And if I were a linnet I would sing my love to rest,
> And if I was a nightingale I would sing till the morning clear,
> I'd sit and sing to you, Polly, for once I loved you dear.[3]

In 2004, Bob received an MBE for his lifelong service to folk music and – comforted by the knowledge that his family's legacy would live on – he made his contribution to Coppers' Corner four days later. His work was done.

In the height of heat one August, I made my way to Rottingdean and was surprised to find it just off the busy A27. After reading about its rural past, I had rather naively expected to find it down some picturesque country lane. With my dad and brother, we parked on the outskirts and walked seaward, past the Copper's flint-bejewelled cottage (now with a blue plaque on the front), and into the High Street. The farm the Coppers worked was split up long ago and sold, and housing once contained to the valley now sprawls over both hillsides.

I stuck my head into The Black Horse, which the owner told me was closed, so instead we bought a local Harvey's Sussex Best from the shop across the road. Birds chirped as we sat on the village green, scorched yellow by the sun, amongst "ducks and drakes" on the village pond. The green next to Kipling's Cottage (where Rudyard Kipling lived for a time) was still chocolate-box pretty, besides the line of parked cars. After spending the afternoon in next-door Brighton, I turned back towards Rottingdean and walked up Beacon Hill, running my hand through long grasses. Reaching the gaunt black windmill at the top, allotments entered the foreground, and behind it stretched the entire valley.

Evening birdsong funnelled through the vale and a sliver of descending blood-orange sun gilded the clouds, aptly signalling "shepherd's delight". Looking onto the village's bursting main road, struggling to accommodate so many cars, a comforting thought surfaced. By continuing to sing and listen to such songs as 'Charming Molly' and 'As I Walked Out', we have the privilege of keeping alive the spirit of long-passed and oft forgotten countryfolk who also sang them, and their unhurried way of life.

> Sweet jug, jug, jug, jug, jug, jug, jug the nightingale did sing,
> Whose noble voice, made all rejoice; as they were hay-making.[4]

\* \* \*

From songs like 'Charming Molly', very much rooted in southern England, we move to 'The Nightingale's Song', later known as 'The Bold Grenadier', which has been collected from both sides of the pond. The earliest known version of this song was published between 1689 and 1709 in a collection of ballads, and over 140 examples were collected from the USA, Canada and England, displaying music's ability to migrate across the Atlantic like a snow bunting from Alaska.

One of the best-known recordings is by The Dubliners, an Irish folk band created in 1962. With his bright ginger afro and voice like a fret board, founding member Luke Kelly was unmistakable in sound and appearance. Before his singing career, he worked in England doing odd jobs like railway cleaning, but an English folk revival was underway, and Luke wanted in. He began frequenting folk clubs with the intention of memorizing as many songs as he could and building up a repertoire.

When he returned to Ireland in the 1960s, Irish folk music was unfashionable, and the bars had a strict attitude of "drink up and shut up." The four founding band members knew each other from various pub gatherings and music events, but everything came together when they started meeting in O'Donoghue's Pub, a black-and-white building with a lustrous woody interior. Performing together as The Ronnie Drew Ballad Group, named after their bearded, piercing-eyed front-man, one auspicious evening they played a few reels on the fiddle and banjo, much to the distaste of the owner. Luke just happened to be reading James Joyce's *Dubliners*, and his copy lay on the counter. The name was perfect.

After signing onto a record label in 1965 and building up their act suitable for concert halls, they began to gain traction, eventually appearing on *Top of the Pops* just two years later. Irish television took a while to acclimatise to the cultural shift presented by The Dubliners. The mood was devout, and everything was done 'properly'. Some could not compute their mixture of smart suits with long hair and unkempt beards, but traditional folk music was well and truly back, and redis-covered ballads like 'The Bold Grenadier' were well received – eventually.

# Singing Like Larks

## The Bold Grenadier

As I went a walking one morning in May,
I met a young couple who so fondly did stray
And one was a young maid so sweet and so fair
And the other was a soldier and a brave grenadier.

*Chorus*:
And they kissed so sweet and comforting as they clung to each
   other.
They went arm in arm along the road like sister and brother.
They went arm in arm along the road 'til they came to a stream,
And they both sat down together love to hear the nightingale sing.
Out of his knapsack he took a fine fiddle
He played her such merry tunes that you ever did hear
He played her such merry tunes that the valley did ring
And softly cried the fair maid as the nightingale sings.

"Oh, I'm off to India for seven long years
Drinking wines and strong whiskies instead of strong beer
And if ever I return again 'twill be in the spring
And we'll both sit down together love to hear the nightingale
   sing."

"Well then", says the fair maid, "Will you marry me?"
"Oh no", says the soldier, "however can that be?"
"For I've my own wife at home in my own country
And she is the finest little maid that you ever did see."

The duality of the nightingale's song rears its head again: beauty and tragedy. At first, the cheerful birdsong seems a fitting soundtrack for a young couple content with each other's company, but oh how the tale turns. By the end, the quavering notes cruelly hit home the unrequited love and slyness of the soldier which leads to their sad separation. Still, the bird remains a constant throughout, a judgeless spectator, and the song continues despite all of the unfortunate goings on. We can take comfort from this. No matter what trials we face in life, the natural world is always there to fall back on, and we can rely on it when we need it most.

Along with 'Sweet Nightingale', this is the second song to feature a similar line to "to hear the nightingale sing". For some, this is a clear euphemism and, although this point is debated, it certainly puts a different spin on the lyrics!

Nightingale songs, like 'The Bold Grenadier', are generally set in May, spring's maturity. This month is a thrumming, buzzing showcase of wildlife when the days lengthen, jumpers come off and trees finish slipping their leafy green coats back on. The nightingale arrives around April and sings until late May or early June, so the use of this accomplished songster in a springtime ballad is a wonderfully descriptive scene-setting tool. The mere mention of a nightingale lifts any song, setting the lyrics into the beating heart of a new beginning.

* * *

There is a Ukrainian folktale telling of how the species began its days in India. One day, a bold nightingale left and flew to Ukraine where, seeing the locals downcast, the bird sang to cheer them up. Now, each year, nightingales are said to visit the country to sing and raise spirits. The nightingale is now the national bird of Ukraine – with *Soloveiko* (nightingale) used as a term of endearment – and Shevchenko, a native nineteenth-century poet, observed that, "Even the memory of the nightingale's song makes man happy."

# Singing Like Larks

How, then, can such exuberant song be heard as a lament? Beauty is in the eye of the beholder, and such interpretations show the extent of humanity's ability to project our own thoughts and feelings onto the natural world – positive and negative. However, the reverse can also be true. The space and scenery found in nature is always there to lift our spirits, if we choose to let it, and very few things can top evening verses from a darkening canopy and – forgathered like traditional singers in the village pub – small birds led in the dusk chorus by sweet nightingales.

Most musical, most melancholy' bird!
A melancholy bird? Oh! Idle thought!
In nature there is nothing melancholy.

Samuel Coleridge, 'The Nightingale: A Conversation Poem'
(1798)

# The Cutty Wren

## (*Troglodytes troglodytes*)

*'Twas on a merry time,*
*when Jenny Wren was young,*
*So neatly as she danced,*
*and so sweetly as she sung*

— 'Cock Robin and Jenny Wren'

BRITAIN'S MOST COMMON breeding bird is small, but mighty. The tiny wren is the abiding rambler's friend, the singer's companion, and has reached the heights of cultural icon.

Gleaming in bronze, a wren adorned the British farthing for much of the twentieth century and, with her tail boldly cocked at eighty degrees, "heads or tails?" has never been more descriptive. Our tiny wren was displayed on one face, and on the obverse was a king. One of the smallest birds is a fitting image to grace one of the smallest-value coins, worth only a quarter of a penny, but the wren means so much more to us than that. Her metallic notes punch well above their weight, in spite of her pocket size, and speak to the very spirit of our small Atlantic isle – courage against all odds.

Walking my dog down nearby Bramble Lane, my eyeline is interrupted by flitting, zipping, horizontal blurs of rufous brown as a wren darts from thicket to thorny thicket. She has been and gone before I can fully process what I have seen and, most of the time, I am completely unaware of her presence. When she sings, the sound reverberating around her delicate frame, I look around for more sizable birds, scarcely able to believe that song of such volume could be produced by such a small creature. With snatches of her song surfacing in my mind, we travel along the lane, catching glimpses of one another as we go.

The alert, mouse-like wren is not Britain's smallest bird, as this prize goes to the minute goldcrest. It does, however, have the loudest song in Britain in proportion to its size. Wrens' explosively delivered melodies sound out all year round from the undergrowth or (less often) from an exposed perch. The sound is punctuated with softer trills, which echo someone running a finger down the back of a deck of cards. Females become fiercely vocal when an intruder, human or otherwise, encroaches on their territory. Perhaps this is why the wren is often called "Jenny" and portrayed as female. This familiar name is thought to have originated in the Middle Ages, alongside her friends Tom Tit, Willy Wagtail, Jack-Daw and others.

The Victorian nursery rhyme 'Cock Robin and Jenny Wren' paints a wonderful picture of Jenny and tells the story of her courtship with a robin. Whilst the song originates from 1877, the notion of a robin marrying a wren is an ancient one, dating back to around 1400. The unknown author encapsulates Victorian polite society in bird form at a time when curiosity about the natural world (especially songbirds) was raging and the keeping of canaries in bird cages or freely flying around the house was popular, as were ditties like this:

Cock Robin and Jenny Wren
'Twas on a merry time,
When Jenny Wren was young,
So neatly as she danced,
And so sweetly as she sung,
Robin Redbreast lost his heart,
He was a gallant bird,
He doffed his cap to Jenny Wren,
Requesting to be heard.

"My dearest Jenny Wren,
If you will but be mine,
You shall dine on cherry pie,
And drink nice currant wine;
I'll dress you like a gold-finch,
Or like a peacock gay,
So if you'll have me, Jenny, dear,
Let us appoint the day."

Jenny blushed behind her fan
And thus declared her mind –
"So let it be to-morrow, Rob,
I'll take your offer kind;
Cherry pie is very good,
And so is currant wine,
But I will wear my plain brown gown,
And never dress too fine."

# Singing Like Larks

Robin Redbreast got up early,
All at the break of day,
He flew to Jenny Wren's house,
And sang a roundelay;
He sang of Robin Redbreast,
And pretty Jenny Wren,
And when he came unto the end,
He then began again.

The modesty of the wren is plain to see, content with her "plain brown gown". Wrens are often entwined with robins in folklore, and multiple phrases lump them together:

Robin redbreast and the wren,
God Almighty's cock and hen.

and –

Kill a robin or a wren,
Never prosper, boy or man.

From Jenny to Jenson, let's move on to a more manly portrayal (not that anyone has actually ever called the wren "Jenson"). In Germany, the wren is portrayed as not only masculine, but a regal winged monarch, known as *Zaun-könig*, translating to "hedge king". This is a far cry from our Jenny Wren, but for many years in Britain and further afield, the wren has been crowned "king of the birds". This traditional folktale tells of the action-filled coronation:

*Many years ago, all the birds of the air gathered together to decide which of them should be king. After much debate, they decided to hold a contest: whichever bird could fly the highest would be king of the birds. On the day of the competition, all the birds took off.*

# The Cutty Wren

Smaller birds quickly tired, their fragile wings unable to carry them high enough. Soon they were joined by ducks, crows and many others. Only the eagles were still able to climb higher into the sky. One eagle in particular climbed higher and higher until the last of his competition gave up and returned to the ground. He congratulated himself smugly and began his descent. But, as he was falling, he heard a small bright voice above him call out "I am king! I am king!". It was a little brown wren, fluttering far above him. She had carefully hidden among the eagle's feathers and ridden on his back, high into the sky.

When the wren landed the small birds cried with joy and surprise. They were certain that one of the larger birds would win the competition but had been too afraid to complain. "You only won through trickery and cunning, and that's not fair," the large birds protested.

"Eagle would have won through strength and brawn. Why is that better than cunning? If you have your doubts name another challenge and I will win once more," the wren replied.

The large birds chatted among themselves and came up with a solution. "We have a new competition. Whichever bird can swoop the lowest will be the king of the birds."

The birds began the new competition, diving down to glide along the ground. Wren saw a small mouse-hole in the earth and climbed into it. She called out "I am king! I am king! I am the lowest!"

The large birds were furious, and decided that the wren could be the king, but she would never rule them. They each took turns standing guard at the hole, waiting to kill the wren if she tried to climb out. Days passed, and the wren stubbornly remained in her hole. One night, an owl was guarding the hole, watching the wren with large yellow eyes. When the morning sunlight peeked over the *horizon, it momentarily blinded the guard and the wren took her chance to escape.*

*The little brown wren remains king of the birds to this very day, but she is so afraid of the eagles and hawks that she stays hidden in hedges and bushes. After all, they will kill her if given half a chance. All the other birds visit her for advice, as she is so clever and cunning.* (TRADITIONAL)

* * *

You've heard of Boxing Day, but have you heard of Wren Day? Across Ireland, parts of Britain and further afield, December 26th was once given over to an ancient festival with antecedents that long predate Christianity, centred around the wren.

"Watch out, watch out, the Wrenboys are about!" This St Stephen's Day tradition varied from place to place, but there was usually a group of Wrenboys, composed of men – young and old – dressed in motley clothing, with painted faces or masks, some wearing full-length oat straw suits, stretching up over their heads and shaped into a corn dolly at the top. They would take a wren – dead or alive – and either tie or nail it to the top of a pole or holly bush decorated with colourful ribbons. They would then proceed to "go on the wran" and loudly parade the unfortunate bird around each house in turn, singing songs, Irish dancing and playing traditional airs on fiddles, bodhráns (an Irish drum), accordions, tin whistles and flutes, demanding some money to "bury the wren".

This begging song, also called a "Wrenboy carol", has a bouncy, lively rhythm. Some Wrenboys would sing it as fast as possible to get from one door to the next, trying to collect as much money as possible, while others sang it slower, more deliberately and in unison. A conglomeration of voices clattered through the streets:

The Wran Song
The wren, the wren, the king of all birds,
St Stephen's Day was caught in the furze,
Although he was little his honour was great,
Jump up me lads and give him a treat.

*Chorus:*
Up with the kettle and down with the pan,
And give us a penny to bury the wren.

As I was going to Killenaule,
I met a wren upon the wall.
I took me stick and knocked him down,
And brought him in to Carrick Town.

Droolin, Droolin, where's your nest?
'Tis in the bush that I love best
In the tree the holly tree,
Where all the boys do follow me.

We followed the wren three miles or more,
Three miles or more three miles or more.
We followed the wren three miles or more,
At six o'clock in the morning.

I have a little box under me arm,
Under me arm under me arm.
I have a little box under me arm,
A penny or tuppence would do it no harm.

# Singing Like Larks

The wren was buried when all of the houses had been visited, sometimes opposite a house that refused to give any food, drink or money to the Wrenboys. This supposedly brought bad luck for the next year.

My first question upon hearing about Wren Day – called *Lá an Dreoilín* in Irish – was: how did they catch a wren in the first place? It was not easy. Days before the noisy procession of song and dance on December 26th, the Wrenboys would venture into the leafless woods and peat bogs and search tirelessly through the thatched roofs of houses with knobbly sticks to hunt for this poor creature. Once they found one, they chased it until either they had caught it, or it died of exhaustion – I am sure many managed to evade them. The 1840 wren hunt in Cork is described in Hall's Ireland, published the following year:

> *For some weeks preceding Christmas, crowds of village boys may be seen peering into the hedges, in search of the "tiny wren"; and when one is discovered the whole assemble and give eager chase to, until they have slain, the little bird. In the hunt, the utmost excitement prevails; shouting, screeching, and rushing; all sorts of missiles are flung at the puny mark; and not unfrequently, they light upon the head of some less innocent being. From bush to bush, from hedge to hedge, is the wren pursued until bagged with as much pride and pleasure, as the cock of the woods by the more ambitious sportsman.*

In Pembrokeshire, Wales, where Wren Day was also celebrated, the hunting of the wren (or *wrenhe*) took place on the Twelfth Night of Christmas. The tiny bird would be caged in a wooden box and carried from door to door, and occupants were asked to pay to peep inside, saying, "Please to see the king." In return for a monetary contribution, little brown wren feathers were given out for good luck. When all the feathers had been given away, the money would go towards a feast and – dizzied with alcohol – the wren's bones were buried, supposedly transferring strength from the king of the birds to the villagers. This Wren Day song was collected from Pembrokeshire:

Joy, Health, Love and Peace
Joy, health, love and peace be all here in this place
By your leave we will sing concerning our king

Our king is well dressed in the silks of the best
We have ribbons so rare, no king can compare

We have travelled many miles over hedges and stiles
In search of our king, unto you we bring

We have powder and shot for to conquer the lot
We have cannon and ball to conquer them all

Now Christmas is past, Twelfth Night is the last,
And we bid you adieu, great joy to the new.

So, what did the innocent wren do to deserve such barbaric persecution? According to Christian folklore, a treacherous wren betrayed the martyr St Stephen by making chattering noises as he was hiding from his enemies in the bush, hence why Wren Day is celebrated on St Stephen's Day in Ireland. Other pagan myths purport that the death of the wren symbolised the death of winter, with the robin supposedly representing the New Year.

The druids – priests, magicians, soothsayers and general repositories of wisdom in the ancient Celtic religion of

Druidry – are said to have killed a wren at the darkest time of year. These people were the intermediaries between this world and the next and used the flight pattern of birds like the wren as auguries. Wren-killing was potentially a continuation of an even older druid tradition of sacrificing the actual king every seven years to maintain the fertility and good of the tribe. Some even believe that the Gaelic word for "wren" – *dreoilín* – derives from two words, *draoi ean*, or "druid bird".

There are many proposed origins of Wren Day but, as is usually the case with folktales and traditions, the true origin probably lies somewhere in between them all.

Wren Day is still observed in Dingle, Co. Kerry (as well as in the Isle of Man and a few other locations), where a vast street parade of straw-covered Wrenboys passes along a street of vibrantly coloured shops and houses towards the Atlantic. The whole town is lifted with musicians' whistles, fife and drums and the heavy shaking of collection boxes – with the money collected now going to charity. Innocent bystanders are swept into the parade and chased down alleyways and, these days, a fake wren is used, with all references to killing the wren being purely symbolic – thank goodness.

By leaving the ritual slaughter in the past, Wren Day has become an animal-friendly occasion on which people unite to bring the traditional Wrenboy carols to life and light up the darkest corner of the year. As they say triumphantly in John Street, Dingle, each Wren Day: "Up *Sraid Eoin*! We never died a winter yet."

When the wheel of life runs down and when peace
   comes over me

34

# The Cutty Wren

O lay me down in that old town between the hills and sea.
I'll take my sleep in those green fields, the place my life began,
Where the boys of Barr na Sráide went hunting for the wran.

– 'The Boys of Barr na Sráide', written by Irish poet Sigerson
Clifford (1913–85) about a street in Cahersiveen, Co. Kerry,
on the southern shore of Dingle Bay.

\* \* \*

I first heard 'The Wran Song' on a recording of the famous Irish
musicians Tommy Makem and The Clancy Brothers performing live in Carnegie Hall, New York, in 1963. With Tommy at
their side, the brothers end their version of 'The Wran Song'
with a verse of their own, much to the delight of their cheering
audiences:

Mrs Clancy's a very good woman,
A very good woman, a very good woman,
Mrs Clancy's a very good woman,
She give us a penny to bury the wren.

Wearing their matching cream knitted Aran sweaters,
contrasting with their short dark hair, the group contributed
immensely to the 1960s folk revival, helping to popularise
Irish music in America and revitalise it in Ireland, where it
had been largely dormant for decades. Their quick wit, charm
and energetic arrangements of old ballads and other songs
brought traditions like Wren Day to a new audience and
made them the most famous musicians in Ireland for a time.
Without them, such folkloric events as the annual Wren Hunt
might have passed me by. Tommy Makem (1932–2007), with

his heavy baritone, recorded nearly two dozen albums with The Clancy Brothers and hailed from a singing family in the small market town of Keady, Co. Armagh – "the Hub of the Universe" as he called it. His father was a fiddler whilst his mother, Sarah Makem (1900–83), was a remarkable ballad singer, and one of the reasons why I cannot work whilst listening to music; if one of her recordings comes on the shuffle, I have to stop and listen. Tommy learnt songs from his parents and older brother Jack, who himself learnt many songs from the wandering musicians who travelled through Ireland attending fairs and ceilidhs.

Like her sons, Sarah was also bred and buttered in thriving Keady, as was her mother before her, surrounded by the tailors, nailers and linen workers who lived there, and the local farmers on market day. Her mother, who worked with the linen, came from the Singing Greenes of Keady, a famous singing family which spanned generations, so Sarah had an excellent teacher growing up. "Sure the girl could sing, she could sing the birds off the bushes. And so could all belonging to her," Sarah once said about her mother.

The house of her childhood was filled with music, and her mother always had a song on her lips. "I was very easily taught a song," Sarah would say, and she would listen to her mother whilst making porridge, baking bread and completing other chores, often picking up the lyrics after hearing them only once, and asking her mother to write down any little bits she did not quite catch. School was also a melting pot of songs as Keady – being on the Northern Irish border – was a place where English, Scottish and Irish songs intermingled.

Filmed in the kitchen of her cottage for a 1977 television

documentary, Sarah's grey hair is neatly pinned back, and she wears a purple-printed paisley knee-length apron. Her sharp blue eyes look through rimless oval glasses. She makes a cup of tea, drops in a teaspoon of sugar with a *clink* on the rim of the mug, all the while crooning in her emotional yet controlled style, paying due diligence to every word. Sitting down on a cushioned wooden chair, she talks to the man behind the camera like an old friend, explaining how she (like most girls in the town) left school as a dark-haired, handsome young lady and went to work long hours in the local factory as a weaver: 7:00 a.m. until 6:30 p.m.

> As I went a-walking one fine summer's morning
> The birds on the branches they sweetly did sing
> The lads and the lassies together were sporting
> Going down to yon factory their work to begin.[5]

Each day left her just enough time to shoot home for "a mouthful of tea" and complete her household chores. After such an exhausting day, many would fall straight to sleep, but Sarah would sing and dance on the street until 10:00 p.m. with local songsters and musicians lilting and playing mouth organs. "Well, at those street parties anyone was likely to be asked for a song, so I always tried to have one or two ready and I kept learning as many as I could from my mother singing around the house." Silhouetted by Keady's wide high street and grey-spired, nineteenth-century stone monument to a local MP, neighbours brought out stools to sit and listen. "We had the time of our lives," she said, "but they don't do that now."

Over the following decades, Sarah built up an incredibly diverse repertoire of over 500 traditional songs.

# Singing Like Larks

In the 1950s, folk song collectors from the United States, like Peter Kennedy, toured Ireland to record its musical heritage in situ, as did Northern Irish school teacher and folk song collector Sean O'Boyle, in an effort to bring old songs to a younger audience. Sarah welcomed them through her door: "You're as welcome as the flowers in May." With Sarah's musical mind akin to a folk song archive, they had stumbled across an unbelievably rich seam.

Kennedy recorded Sarah in her cottage in 1952 using a portable magnetic tape machine and, since she could best remember songs whilst working, he would follow her around with the microphone, from the kitchen sink to the range and then back again. Her husband would inevitably start up on the fiddle, young Tommy would quietly listen, propped up in the corner, and neighbours and friends would start to move in for a ceilidh (house-visiting party) at the sound of her voice. Nobody could have predicted where these field recordings would end up...

One of the songs that Sarah sang, 'As I Roved Out', became the signature tune of a Sunday morning BBC Radio programme of the same title which ran right through the fifties. Having never left her beloved hometown, Sarah was the last person to expect one million households to be awoken by her voice each week, singing the opening verse, before the tune of the chorus was taken up by a small orchestra.

As I roved out on a May morning
On a May morning right early...

After that, people flocked from miles around to hear her sing, and her voice became known wherever it travelled across the airwaves. In the 1977 documentary, sat in that very same cottage years later, and probably in the exact same wooden chair in the kitchen where the recordings took place, her face lit up at the memory of it all. In a time before social media, when everyday people simply did not receive 'likes' or have thousands of 'followers', Sarah was amazed by the attention and, in slight disbelief, she said with a smile, "If I had of know'd it was going out to all them people, I would have never opened my mouth!"

As a private and unboastful person, Sarah was content for her songs to stay in and around Keady. But, like the humble Jenny Wren hiding herself away in bracken, bush and briar, she possessed talents too immeasurably valuable to go unheard. Some talents simply have to be shared and, be it from inside a wren's bush or Sarah's little cottage, their songs are renowned the world over.

\* \* \*

A song that has perplexed me since I first came across it is 'The Cutty Wren', with "cutty" being a dialect word meaning "small" or "short" in Northern England and the Scottish Lowlands. It stays true to the hunting theme seen in Wrenboy carols, but has a strange, magical, fairy-tale quality which throws the lyrics wide open to interpretation. The earliest known written version of the rhyme (labelled a lullaby by some) dates from a 1776 book called *Scots Songs*, although it is thought to be far older:

The Cutty Wren

"O where are you going?" said Milder to Maulder
"O we may not tell you," said Festle to Foes
"We're off to the woods," said John the Red Nose.

# Singing Like Larks

"What will you do there?" said Milder to Maulder
"O we may not tell you," said Festle to Foes
"We'll hunt the Cutty Wren," said John the Red Nose.

"How will you shoot her?" said Milder to Maulder
"O we may not tell you," said Festle to Foes
"With bows and with arrows," said John the Red Nose.

"That will not do then," said Milder to Maulder
"O what will do then?" said Festle to Foes
"Big guns and big cannons," said John the Red Nose.

"How will you bring her home?" said Milder to Maulder
"O we may not tell you," said Festle to Foes
"On four strong men's shoulders," said John the Red Nose.

"That will not do then," said Milder to Maulder
"O what will do then?" said Festle to Foes
"Big carts and big waggons," said John the Red Nose.

"How will you cut her up?" said Milder to Maulder
"O we may not tell you," said Festle to Foes
"With knives and with forks," said John the Red Nose.

"That will not do then," said Milder to Maulder
"O what will do then?" said Festle to Foes
"Big hatchets and cleavers," said John the Red Nose.

"Who'll get the spare ribs?" said Milder to Maulder
"O we may not tell you," said Festle to Foes
"We'll give them all to the poor," said John the Red Nose.

This song has been attributed to the end of the fourteenth century, when revolution was in the air. The Peasants Revolt of 1381, also known as Wat Tyler's Rebellion, saw riots in southern

England triggered by socio-economic and political tensions, including high taxes and a long conflict with France during the Hundred Years' War. All of this unrest was further exacerbated by the Black Death in the 1340s. Poverty, sickness and death were rife. To say it was a difficult time would be an understatement.

A diminutive bird rising up to become king of the birds was a well-known story, and it likely adopted a symbolic meaning for rebels. To speak their minds outright would have been tantamount to high treason, punishable by death, so many hid their resentment and discontent in songs and rhymes like this. The cutty wren has been rumoured to represent a young King Richard II, the monarch at the time. The harmless bird is slain like a tyrant, and shared out, as rebels thought the crown's wealth and property should be fairly shared out amongst the poor. It may also comment on food shortages at the time. There is an irony in the characters divvying up parts of the wren using axe-like knives as if the bird amounts to a feast, and still only the pin-like spare ribs go to the poor.

* * *

The songs in this chapter unearth the profound effect that the wren has had, and continues to have, on us. Igniting our imagination, their larger-than-life role in folklore and song takes some weird and wild turns, from the beloved wife of the robin, to a king, to a hunted traitor. But, putting all of that to one side, there is one lesson to be learnt from Jenny Wren: it matters not how big you are, but how loudly your heart sings.

# Up with the Larks

## (*Alauda arvensis*)

*As I hear the sweet lark sing*
*In the clear air of the day.*

– 'The Lark in the Clear Air'

ARE YOU A MORNING LARK, or a night owl? I would have to confess to being the latter, but it is certainly true that larks rise early. The lark, and by that I refer mainly to the skylark, sings to the first light of dawn and – what's more – they sing as they fly. Spending much of their time exactly where the name suggests, high up in the sky, they are unapologetically conspicuous, out-pouring an effortless liquid warble on the wing.

Larks mainly sing during their display flights, beginning as winter comes to an end and persisting throughout the breeding season. Their jumble of chirrups starts just after lifting off from the ground, rising almost vertically to fifty metres or more and hovering, hanging in the air like a dust spot and beating their wings at ten to twelve beats per second. Finger-like tail feathers fan out behind and creamy-tan underwings flow from a streaky brown throat. Continuing to rise, they can sometimes reach 300 metres! Singing sustained and complicated songs, this aerial musical mesmerises potential mates and strengthens existing pair bonds. When the show is over – sometimes lasting as long as an hour – they fall silent, returning to earth in leisurely fashion.

The song of the lark mimics and incorporates songs from other birds, particularly waders like the curlew, which is no different from folk music. Traditional songs are constantly evolving, merging with each other, and one song can diverge into two entirely different entities, or three, or four! An individual will, perhaps without even thinking, alter a song in melody, rhythm and lyrics to satisfy their own personal artistry. The lark certainly does this too.

Larks feature in countless traditional folk songs, but why? To find out, we first need to look to history. As our ancestors cleared forests and other habitats to make way for pasture and farmland, the lark followed along with them. Their diet is mapped upon the farming calendar with cereal grain and weed seeds in autumn, seeds in winter, newly sown grain in spring and insects in summer as the crops are growing. Hopping along the ground, they search and dig, with just their browny-black crest poking up out of the grass (what a cool hairdo). Since these changes in land use, the lark has been ever-present in farm and grasslands, and their determined song has become a quintessential sound of the countryside.

One man well acquainted with the song of the lark was George "Pop" Maynard. Born the eleventh of twelve children on January 6th, 1872 – "Old Christmas Day" as he called it – Pop was a lifelong Sussex farmworker and lover of old songs.

# Singing Like Larks

Attending school on and off until the age of twelve in the small village of Copthorne – where he lived his whole life – Pop worked with his father and brothers as a woodsman in winter, cutting wood for the hoop trade, and in summer helped with harvesting, hedging and ditching.

Pop learnt songs from broadsides (sometimes known as song sheets or broadsheets: a single sheet of inexpensive paper with a ballad, news and sometimes a woodcut illustration), which were hawked around the villages by pedlars, along with cheap jewellery and ribbons. For fifty-two years, without fail, Pop travelled to the dusty fields of Kent for seasonal work in the hop fields, learning songs from itinerant workers as they harvested. Singing was part of everyday life, at work and play, as he attests: "Everybody sang. Some sang well, some didn't, but singing was as normal as breathing. We sang up in the woods, we sang everywhere."

However, the main avenue through which Pop learnt traditional songs was from older members of his family whilst growing up. In a recording made in his local pub, the Cherry Tree, when he was an old man – the noisy chatter and playing of shove ha'penny and darts dies into a few background coughs – he says, "I'll try one what my father used to sing. He learnt it off his father." It goes like this:

Ground for the Floor *(the last two lines of each verse repeat)*
The sun being set and my work it is done.
One more of my days I have spent.
Through the meadows to my cottage I tripp–ed along
And I set myself down with content.

My cottage with woodbine are deckèd all round.
I've just only green at my door.

# Up with the Larks

Where in it there's no trouble nor care to be found.
Oh, I've nothing but ground for my floor.

My bed's made of flock and my sheets they're home-spun.
No trouble ever enters my breast.
At night when I'm weary, I lay myself down
And so sweetly I there take my rest.

Like a lark in the morning I rise to my work.
There is nothing perplexing my mind.
If a lamb goes astray, I'll so carefully look.
If I seek, I am sure for to find

My pipe's made of straw. For an minute I play,
While the lambkins leap over the plain.
I am blessed with content. How my time slips away,
And at night to my cottage again.

No thoughts about riches never entered my breast.
Nor none of their honours I desire.
For the chiefest of my studies in earning of my bread
And proud title I never could admire.

*Spoken:* "That's all I know of it."

Unafraid to hold notes – "like a laaaark in the moorning" –
Pop's voice wobbles in an emotive vibrato, and his rich Sussex
dialect flavours every word. Repeating the last two lines of
each verse, the whole pub begins to join in until the end, when
the recording erupts with applause and shouts of "Well done,
Pop!" – no doubt accompanied by pats on the back. This exact
recording can be heard on an anthology album of traditional
working men and women, called *There Is a Man Upon the
Farm – The Voice of the People, Vol* 20 (Topic Records, 1998).

# Singing Like Larks

Having learnt most of his songs from the oral tradition, Pop attracted the attention of folk song collectors during the second folk song revival in the 1950s and was recorded multiple times during the last ten years of his life – including three times for the BBC. In his old age he was trim and wore a flat cap. His high, bulbous cheeks almost buried his deep-set eyes when he smiled – which he often did – and his bushy white beard covered his neckerchief. A chain hung down his front, connected to a watch in his waistcoat pocket. He was a character, and it was not only his singing that made him a local celebrity, but something else entirely: marbles.

Pop led the Copthorne Spitfires to victory as team captain at the 1948 British and World Marbles Championship, and he earned his nickname, "Pop", for the skilful way in which he squeezed marbles between thumb and finger to pop them out at high speed.

In Pop's final year before his passing in 1962, he could still be seen down in the Cherry Tree pub, telling stories and singing songs with his crackling voice, banging his stick to keep in time with the music. He was "a complete countryman" and sang songs like 'Ground for the Floor' until the end, a testament to his lark-filled days in the Sussex grasslands and Kentish hop fields.

\* \* \*

A better-known traditional song is 'The Lark in the Morning', popular across the British Isles, although twenty-eight out of the thirty-seven recorded versions come from England. The earliest known version was published in a garland (or "chapbook") – a folded broadside containing a number of songs

– called *Four Excellent New Songs*, printed in Edinburgh in 1778. Chapbooks were an inexpensive form of literature in the eighteenth and nineteenth centuries, and pedlars would buy them in bulk as un-made-up sheets and walk around the country selling, binding and ofttimes colouring them en route to the next village fair. If a local place name appeared in a song, they would simply change it to relate to their next audience.

'The Lark in the Morning' was regularly printed in broadsides throughout the nineteenth century. Here are the lyrics as sung by Bob and Ron Copper, recorded by Peter Kennedy, highlighting the lark's virtuosity:

### The Lark in the Morning
The lark in the morning she arises from her nest
And she ascends all in the air with the dew upon her breast,
And with the pretty ploughboy she'll whistle and she'll sing,
And at night she'll return to her own nest again.

When his day's work is over, oh, what then will he do?
Perhaps then into some rude country wake he'll go,
And with his pretty sweetheart he'll dance and he'll sing,
And at night he'll return with his love back again.

And as they return from the wake unto the town,
The meadows they are mowed and the grass it is cut down.
The nightingale she whistles upon the hawthorn spray,
And the moon it is a-shining upon the new-mown hay.

Good luck unto the ploughboys, wherever they may be.
They will take a winsome lass for to sit upon their knee,
And with a jug of beer, boys, they'll whistle and they'll sing,
And the ploughboy is as happy as a prince or a king.

# Singing Like Larks

A variant of this song was collected in Herongate, Essex, by the eminent composer Ralph Vaughan Williams (1872–1958) in 1904 from a Mr Kemp. It begins with a conversation between a shepherd and his wife, Floro, as she tries to persuade him on one cold morning to stay in bed a little longer, but he shows his resolve:

> "Lay still my fond shepherd and don't you rise yet
> It's a fine dewy morning and besides, my love, it is wet."
> "Oh let it be wet my love and ever so cold
> I will rise my fond Floro and away to my fold."
>
> "Oh no, my bright Floro, it is no such thing
> It's a bright sun a-shining and the lark is on the wing."

This shepherd's resilience is mirrored in the lark's song which, when heard, seems to go on without end. Although it may seem endless, what sounds like the continuous song of one lark is usually the songs of many. Each bird's spirited performance rarely lasts for more than five minutes, but as one song terminates, another rises swiftly into the sky from a contiguous grassy territory and broadcasts its own composition to fill the gap. Perhaps this shared drive also explains why the lark pops up in songs of the tireless shepherd and bonny ploughboy.

'The Lark in the Morning' remains a favourite in the folk community today, performed by The Dubliners, Steeleye Span, Maddie Prior, Magpie Lane and many more. However, my favourite rendition is by an Irish traditional folk singer and raconteur called Paddy Tunney (1921–2002), affectionately known as "The Man of Songs." A love of traditional music ran in the Tunney family, and they accrued a huge stock of songs. Although he was born in Glasgow, the family returned to Paddy's maternal grandfather's cottage in Rusheen, Co. Donegal, within a few weeks of his birth. Paddy's first song teacher was his grandfather and, out of all the thousands of songs in existence, the very first one he was taught when he was just four years old was 'The Lark in the Morning'. His version begins like most others, but ends with an entirely different verse:

Roger the ploughboy he is a bonnie blade,
He goes whistling and singing by yonder lone shade.
He met with dark-eyed Susan, she's handsome I declare,
And she's far more enticing than the birds of the air.
He met with dark-eyed Susan, she's handsome I declare,
And he bought for her some ribbons for to roll round her hair.

In some recordings, Paddy finishes by lilting – a traditional form of Celtic singing, sometimes called "mouth music" or "diddling". Everyone's lilt is different, with an array of di-dl-ee-die-dum sounds, in different orders. Some historians believe that this form of music arose centuries ago among the peasantry due to the unavailability of instruments (although it is unclear exactly when this might have happened). It is a fast-paced, difficult skill to master, and I have tripped over my tongue countless times trying to sing along with Paddy. Many of his songs featured birds, including one of my favourites called 'Moorlough Mary', in which the singer is trying to woo his love, and the lark has some avian company:

Moorlough Mary *(verses 2–4)*
Were I a man of great education
Or Erin's Isle at my own command,
I would lay my head on your snowy bosom,
In wedlock bands, love, we'd join our hands.

# Singing Like Larks

I would entertain you both night and morning,
With robes I'd deck you both night and day,
And with kisses sweet, love, I would embrace you;
O Moorlough Mary, won't you come away?

On Moorlough's banks, now, no more I'll wander
Where heifers graze on yon pleasant soil,
Where lambkins sporting, fair maids resorting,
The timorous hare and blue heather bell;
I would press my cheese while my wool's a-teasing,
My ewes I'd milk by the break of day,
While the whirring moorcock and lark allures me,
O Moorlough Mary, won't you come away?

Now I'll away to my situation,
My recreation is all in vain;
On the River Mourne where the salmon's sporting,
The rocks re-echoing my plaintive strain;
Where the thrush and blackbird do join harmonious,
Their notes melodious on the river brae,
And the little song-birds will join in chorus:
"O Moorlough Mary, won't you come away?"

* * *

Vaughan Williams may have collected 'The Lark in the Morning', but it is not the symphonist's only link with the lark – not by a long chalk. He composed *The Lark Ascending* in 1914. It is not a folk song, but rather a contemplative classical piece which has entered Britain's musical hall of fame. Within its bars, the violin is transformed into a songster in flight, rising higher and higher, and then falling delicately through the air, in time with the changing melody. The sound of the bow dancing across the strings brings to life dramatic images of the chirruping lark flying over familiar fields.

Written against the backdrop of World War I, a lingering sadness clings to the music, redolent of untimely death and widespread mechanisation. The skylark became a symbol of Mother Nature and her ability to persist through barbaric destruction. Multiple soldiers' diaries and letters are filled with songful observations of the lark energetically trilling overhead but rendered voiceless through the inferno of artillery fire. Eyes turned from the miserable trenches to the sky, war poet Isaac Rosenberg wrote, "Heights of night ringing with unseen larks: / Music showering on our upturned faces". He was sadly killed in 1918, but the skylark reminded men like Isaac of home; a comforting reminder that survival, however unlikely, was possible.

At the head of the original score, written with a pencil in flowing cursive, is the title 'The Lark Ascending – Romance for Violin and Orchestra' and underneath Vaughan Williams reveals the inspiration for this musical revelation – George Meredith's 1881 poem of the same name. The score sheet is scribbly and draft-like, with only twelve lines included, and four lines crossed out:

The Lark Ascending
He rises and begins to round,
He drops the silver chain of sound,
Of many links without a break,
In chirrup, whistle, slur and shake,

For singing till his heaven fills,
'Tis love of earth that he instils
And ever winging up and up,
Our valley is his golden cup,

# Singing Like Larks

And he the wine which overflows
To lift us with him as he goes;
He is, the dance of children, thanks
Of sowers, shout of primrose banks,
And eye of violets while they breathe;
All these the circling song will wreathe...
Till lost on his aërial rings
In light ... and then the fancy sings.

The earthy composition was an immediate hit, with a critic from *The Times* noting that, like a folk song, "the music is of the clean countryside, not of the sophisticated concert-room." To this day, it transports listeners high into the speckled blue sky and all the way down to the seed-blown, leaf-laden grasslands of England – illustrating Meredith's poem time and again.

Vaughan Williams was heavily inspired by traditional folk music and for ten years he devoted up to thirty days a year collecting songs from singers in twenty-one English counties. He arranged many traditional songs into classical styles, creating his *English Folk Song Suite,* and he even composed folk melodies of his own. Like many of the song-collecting pioneers of the nineteenth century, Vaughan Williams understood that a musical tradition was being lost and rural songs were no longer being passed on. I can hear this in *The Lark Ascending:* the ecstatic rolling beauty of the British countryside, with its apricot sunrises burnishing hummocky grounds of wheat-stem gold and vegetable green, dissected by puddled tracks where countryfolk nod their heads at each other as they pass. Tucked deep in the troughs of the tune, the violin morosely cries out against the loss of that vision, the mislaying of a wilder mindset and its music.

Brisk and Bonny Lad[6]
I am a brisk and bonny lad and free from care and strife
And sweetly as the hours pass I love a country life.
At wake or fair I'm often there 'midst pleasure to be seen,
Though poor I am contented and as happy as a Queen.

I rise up in the morning my labour to pursue
And with my yoke and milking pails I trudge the morning dew.
My cows I milk and then I taste how sweet the nature yields,
The lark she sings to welcome me across the flowery fields.

And in the time of harvest how cheerfully we go,
Some with hooks and some with crooks and some with scythes
    to mow.
And when our corn is free from harm we have not far to roam,
We'll all away to celebrate the welcome Harvest Home.

* * *

In September 2021, I found myself just north of the River
Blackwater for a fortnight-long Forest School leadership course
with Essex Wildlife Trust. Forest School, for readers who have
never heard the term, is a kind of outdoor, nature-based learning for children, including activities like fire lighting, whittling,
tool use, den building and bug hunting – similar to the Scouts
but with a focus on the environment.

On the horizon, rusty marshes curled left and right in a
tessellating brain-like structure around a bright, red-hulled
lightship, and the sunlight danced off quartzy silt. A mile or
so inland, I was in a world of colour with the sun scattering
her coins of light through a copse of horse chestnut and oak.
English ivy caught the wind and mimicked the flapping sails

in the nearby estuary. Three of us were sat around a log circle, close to a fire which slowly smoke-cured my rucksack and raincoat throughout the day. It was here, making polite conversation, that I stumbled into an anecdote too good not to share.

I had just finished whittling a mushroom, which is what I assured everyone else it was after a few playful sideways looks! The fire spat and a long, concentrated silence passed before one of the women asked what I was up to at the moment. I mentioned that I was planning on writing this book, still an embryo of an idea, to which a shy, dark-haired lady who we can call "Anna" immediately responded, "Will you have a chapter on the skylark?"

"Oh yes, for sure," I replied. "The book wouldn't be complete without it."

Anna's face lit up as bright as the embers floating up into the canopy. She explained that, aged fourteen, she fell on the school playground, hitting her head on a concrete path. She suffered from long-term memory loss and severe insomnia as a result. After months of misery, Anna discovered that the only thing soothing enough to get her to sleep was listening to *The Lark Ascending*, its rises and falls vivid enough to stir comforting dreams of the countryside. I took Anna's story home with me that day in my smoke-scented car, as well as a tin bursting with freshly fallen conkers for my Forest School – they have many uses.

* * *

Our memories are notoriously unreliable. Upon hearing a song, over time we are liable to forget lyrics or even whole verses. New words are subsequently made up and substituted, meaning that folk songs are constantly in flux – forever being moulded and remoulded. Passing through generations of singers – each with their own creative flair – clumsy, hard to remember lines and awkward word choices are slowly sieved out as they fall through the great filter of time, allowing a song to be refined, distilled and concentrated until only the pure essence of subject and sentiment remains. Through this intergenerational process, lyrics may come to possess a curious air of perfection.

Few places did songs change more than at agricultural fairs before the twentieth century. These bustling events were song-swapping hubs, with farmers coming together from all over. Bob Copper had a shepherding uncle called John Copper (c. 1879–1952) who was known for his ability to "capture" a song after hearing it once or twice. John couldn't wait to come home from a sheep fair and share a song which he had heard with Bob's father, Jim, saying, "What do you think of this one, old brother?" John's tip is that he would remember the tune and basic story arc rather than focusing on every word. If a verse or two evaded him when he got home, he would simply fill in the gaps himself. As Bob commented, "You're not gonna lose a good song over a couple lines of words, so you'd put in your own to fill it up and make it good."

Fudging words was, and perhaps still is, common practice, although I suspect less so now that most traditional lyrics are immortalised online. Nevertheless, misremembering lines and singers putting their own artistic spin on certain lines are surely responsible for the multiple variations of some songs; a collaborative editing process, carried out across the centuries, with the ability to lift a piece to heights unimagined by its original author.

It is therefore remarkable when a song written relatively recently is fast-tracked into the tradition, seamlessly entering the ranks of centuries-old songs, without the multitude of alterations, tweaks and evolutions that comes with them. This is certainly the case for Belfast writer Sir Samuel Ferguson's (1810–86) romantic creation, 'The Lark in the Clear Air'.

The Lark in the Clear Air
Dear thoughts are in my mind
And my soul soars enchanted,
As I hear the sweet lark sing
In the clear air of the day.
For a tender beaming smile
To my hope has been granted,
And tomorrow she shall hear
All my fond heart would say.

I shall tell her all my love,
All my soul's adoration;
And I think that she will hear me
And will not say me nay.
It is this that fills my soul
With its joyous elation,
As I hear the sweet lark sing
In the clear air of the day.

The words feel old, like they have always been written, held within the face of a stone like an undiscovered fossil, waiting to be cracked open with a geologist's hammer. Perhaps what has allowed this nineteenth-century song to ingratiate itself with far older works is its tune, which also accompanies an eighteenth-century rebel song. Traditional or not, 'The Lark in the Clear Air' has a classic Irish melody and succinct lyrics which have remained popular since it was authored.

* * *

Singing high and searching low, the lark's playful spiralling behaviour has shaped parts of the English language outside of the folk music sphere. Take the phrase "larking about", for example. Children scavenging on the muddy shorelines of the UK, like a lark hopping around a field for seeds, were called "mudlarks", and the activity is still called "mudlarking" today. Likewise, naval dictionaries reveal that young lads playing around high up in the grey mist-clung rigging of ships were once called "skylarks" by sailors.

This theme of youth and playfulness is continued in folk-lore where larks represent young love as well as daybreak, which they sing through. Multiple wordsmiths have employed the lark for these symbolic purposes, with Chaucer in 'The Knight's Tale' (the first of *The Canterbury Tales*) writing in the fourteenth century:

> The bisy larke: messenger of day, saluted with her song the gray morning.

And Shakespeare in the lamenting 'Sonnet 29' (9–12):

> Yet in these thoughts myself almost despising,
> Haply I think on thee, and then my state,
> Like to the lark at break of day arising
> From sullen earth, sings hymns at heaven's gate.

Young love forms the foundation of the unaccompanied folk song 'Sweet Lemeney', another from the repertoire of the Copper Family, although widely collected around southern Britain. The name "Lemeney", also spelt "Lemody", "Limady" and even "Lemonday", has appeared in many nineteenth-century broad-sides. Thought by many to be simply a picturesque name for the girl in the song, perhaps it was chosen because "lemen" (or "leman") is an archaic word for "lover" or "sweetheart", which makes perfect sense in the context of this romantic song.

I love the raw emotion in the lyrics, the complex melody, and the way the story slowly builds. It was one of the first traditional songs that I heard – first from Bob Copper's daughter, Jill Copper, and then from rough, weatherworn elderly men in early twentieth-century recordings, balancing on each line with thoughtful, reverential poise. Such sounds are striking indeed.

Sweet Lemeney
As I was a-walking one fine summer's morning,
The fields and the meadows they looked so green and gay;
And the birds they were singing so pleasantly adorning,
So early in the morning at the break of the day.

Oh hark, oh hark, how the nightingale is singing,
The lark she is taking her flight all in the air.
On yonder green bower the turtle doves are building,
The sun is just a-glimmering. Arise my dear.

Arise, oh, arise and get your humble posies,
For they are the finest flowers that grow in yonder grove.
And I will pluck them all sweet lily, pink and roses,
All for Sweet Lemeney, the girl that I love.

Oh, Lemeney, oh, Lemeney, you are the fairest creature,
You are the fairest creature that ever my eyes did see.
And then she played it over all on the pipes of ivory,
So early in the morning at the break of the day.

Oh, how could my true love, how could she vanish from me?
Oh, how could she go and I never shall see her more?
But it was her cruel parents that looked so slightly on me,
All for the white robe that I once used to wear.

Here, the lark not only represents the breaking dawn, when he serves as a committed chorist, but also church services, illuminating why he is included in a song about a potential marriage prevented by the daughter's parents. The origins of 'Sweet Lemeney' are obscure, with some folk historians suggesting it could be from an eighteenth-century stage production, while the mention of a "white robe" hints that there may have been far more to the story which has been lost through time. This "white robe" reference may have been readily understood by audiences in days gone by. Is the jilted singer a vicar? A monk? We may never know – it is a folk mystery.

What we do know is that the image of the lark has not changed much. They remain our mid-summertime symbol of light.

\* \* \*

*"How cold it is," said the Snow Man. The local boys had made him the night before, with two bits of slate for eyes and an old rake in his mouth for teeth. How he wished that he could move. One morning, a black dog walked past, saying, "Don't worry Mr. Snow Man, the sun will soon teach you to run."*

*"Thank you," said the Snow Man.*

*The sun rose higher and higher, and the trees – once heavy with snow – began to drip, drip, drip.*

*"Is it not a pretty sight!?" said a little girl, as she looked out of her window.*

*It was a warmer day than yesterday and very soon the poor Snow Man went down, down and never said a word. By early-afternoon he was quite gone.*

*"Poor man," said the dog, "I am sorry for him."*

*Before long the springtime came, and with it the birds and the*

# Singing Like Larks

*flowers. No one thought of the poor Snow Man, and the little girl sang,*

> *"Woods, your nice green dress put on!*
> *Willows, your woolly gloves put on!*
> *Lark and Cuckoo, gaily sing,*
> *February has brought us Spring!*
> *My heart joins in your song so sweet.*
> *Come out, dear Sun, the world to greet."*

A version of this timeless story, *The Snow Man*, is included in the beautifully illustrated book, *The Snow Man and other stories*, edited by Andrew Lang and published in New York in 1903. The stories are based on tales – fairy and otherwise – found in older books and within the oral tradition. As we have already seen from Chaucer and Shakespeare, and now from this wistful story, the lark has inspired nature-loving storytellers since the day we first heard them singing. One of the most famous is Percy Bysshe Shelley's poem, 'To a Skylark' (1820), which begins:

> To a Skylark *(extract)*
> Hail to thee, blithe Spirit!
> Bird thou never wert,
> That from Heaven, or near it,
> Pourest thy full heart
> In profuse strains of unpremeditated art.

The inspiration for this poem is exotic. With his wife, legendary writer Mary Shelley, Percy Bysshe Shelley wandered the Tuscan countryside in rural Italy. They were backdropped by a tomato-hued late-day sky, tall olive trees darkening in the distance, when they heard it. Mary describes the scene: "It was a beautiful summer evening while wandering among the lanes whose myrtle hedges were the bowers of the fire-flies, that we heard the carolling of the skylark." With the upward-flicking crest on the lark's head likened to the "silver sphere" moon, he is lifted to spiritual, otherworldly heights.

Shelley's 'To a Skylark' was paired with Keats' 'Ode to a Nightingale' in 1906 by Scottish academic Alexander Mackie, presented as the two sparkling gems of English literature – day and night symbolised together. Mackie justifies his bold claim by stating that "both were written by men who had no claim to special or exact knowledge of ornithology as such." Indeed, practically all the traditional folk songs in this book were not written, nor sung, by bird experts. That is the beauty of it. Birds can be appreciated by anybody, anywhere. No money, no experience, no identification guides – no problem. All we need is an undisturbed minute.

* * *

When Jones's Ale Was New *(verses 1–2)*
Come all you honest labouring men that work hard all the day
And join with me at the Barley Mow to pass an hour away.
Where we can sing and drink and be merry
And drive away all our cares and worry,
When Jones's ale was new, my boys, when Jones's ale was new.

The first to come in was the ploughman with sweat all on his brow,
Up with the lark at the break of day he guides the speedy plough.
He drives his team, how they do toil
O'er hill and valley to turn the soil,
When Jones's ale was new, my boys, when Jones's ale was new.

# Singing Like Larks

The natural world described in many traditional folk songs is disappearing fast. During the 1990s, the UK lark population halved, even in its preferred farmland habitats. Currently, it has a "red" conservation status. The RSPB posit that this decline may be due to a switch from spring to autumn-sown cereal crops, which are taller and denser, causing fewer birds to nest among them. When nests are built, they are usually close to tramlines – tractor tracks in a field used to apply spray to crops – making nesting larks an easy meal for hungry foxes and other ground predators. Overgrazing in grassland habitats also threatens the skylark as it leaves the grass too short for skylarks to nest, and when they do they are at risk of trampling by cattle and other large animals.

Similarly, over-wintered stubbles, the part of a plant left after the seed has been harvested, provide vital shelter and food in the way of seeds and weeds for the lark. These are traditionally removed after harvest to make way for other crops such as winter barley, leaving little sustenance in late winter, or a seasonal 'food gap'. Leaving stubbles alone over the winter not only helps seed-reliant birds but also reduces soil erosion.

We must face facts. The lark, poster bird for British farmland, finds the current state of agriculture inhospitable.

Maddy Holland released a passionate song called 'A Place Called England' in the 1990s, where the singer rides out in search of a wild England she once knew: "Couldn't find the old flood meadow or the house that I once knew; / No trace of the little river or the garden where I grew." Unable to find it, the singer calls for a triumphant return to "blackbird singing from the May tree, lark ascending through the scales, / Robin watching from your spade and English earth beneath your nails".

# Up with the Larks

We are on the path back to that England described by Holland, and things are looking more positive in Britain as a whole. Farmers are already working alongside the RSPB and the BTO to restore nesting habitats and food resources, giving the lark and its iconic song the breathing space to make a comeback.

Just one example is Lark Rise Farm, 400 acres of wildlife wonder on the outskirts of Cambridge which all began with the purchase of one small field in 1993. The arable fields are awash with colourful wildflowers in summer and butterflies fly like confetti. The owners have managed to transform an intensively farmed wildlife desert into a haven for nature using wildlife-friendly farming methods such as smaller field sizes, crop rotation, leaving over-wintering stubble, beetle banks and wildlife strips. Not only that, but they have also planted 4.5 miles of new hedgerow, all with the help of volunteers.

For their incredible efforts, Lark Rise Farm received a Redlist Revival Award for 'Highest Density of Grey Partridge', while female brown hares box in the springtime fields and water voles burrow nest chambers into the banks of the brook. It truly is nature-rich. Many other Redlist species of conservation concern call the farm home including the song thrush, yellowhammer, linnet and – true to the farm's name – there is an abundance of skylarks.

* * *

In summer, the heathered hills of the Long Mynd turn purple. Grey tors of the quartzite Stiperstones stick jaggedly up to the west like a dinosaur's back. Together, these two formations form the heart of the Shropshire Hills. A sea of bell heather carpets the land, edging right up to footpaths, and each flower looks set to ring. Panoramic views of chessboard-like farmland extend across to Wales on one side and to England on the other, but manmade borders mean little up there, on that long plateau where cultures overlap.

In 2021, the Field Studies Council ran a "Young Darwin Scholarship", offering young naturalists the chance to develop their field skills and meet other like-minded young people. One of the scholarships was based at FSC Preston Montford, a historic house in Shropshire. I was lucky enough to secure a place on the trip where we were taught practical conservation skills like insect and plant identification, small mammal trapping and enjoyed a walk on the Stiperstones.

As the group walked in a long snaking line along the narrow dirt path, chatting about the future of wildlife conservation in the UK, the mood was sunny and hopeful – just like the weather. We got closer and closer to a grey-haired Natural England ranger at the top of the hill, leaning with one foot against the tyre of his army-green Land Rover. Finally reaching him, we sat cross-legged, surrounded by heather, and were handed maps showing the upland areas already managed, the areas recently bought, and the areas of nature-deprived farmland that Natural England intend to purchase, stretching far into the valley. "We want to connect the purple," he said.

After sitting below the stones for some nature journaling and a dramatic reading from *Folk Stories of Shropshire*, a quiet took over. We were all immersed in the scenic majesty, fingers stained slate blue by foraged bilberries (known locally as "whinberries"), when a bulky skylark ascended from the heather to my left, raising a short, reedy volley of calls. Then it was gone.

# Up with the Larks

A fleeting encounter, but every witness was bolstered by this show of flight. Smiling faces looked around at each other with wide-eyed excitement. We were shown exactly what we must protect, and exactly why.

> Come all jolly fellows who delight in being mellow
> Attend unto me and sit easy
> For a pint when it's quiet, my lads, let us try it
> For thinking will drive a man crazy.
>
> I have lawns, I have bowers, I have fruit, I have flowers
> And the lark is my daily alarmer
> So my jolly boys now, here's God speed the plough
> Long life and success to the farmer.
>
> —'The Farmer's Toast', excerpt

# Robert Redbreast

## (*Erithacus rubecula*)

*There came to my window one morning in spring*
*A sweet little robin, she came there to sing*

– 'The Robin'

THIRTEEN MONTHS. On average, and taking into account high mortality rates in the first year, that is the amount of time a robin gets to live; not very long for one of the nation's most-loved birds.

Autumn song flows out of them, riding melancholy on the gathering mists of shortening days, vibrating through the weighted boughs of newly ripened fruit trees. Even in the frozen winter, they will sing just to hold onto feeding territories. From some concealed perch, a more upbeat tune rings out in spring, delivered with the desire to find a mate. In fact, the only time when the robin stops singing is late summer, whilst they moult.

Despite their small stature and fluffy appearance, they are bursting with aggression. Neighbouring pairs play a brutal game of sorts, a deadly dance. Higher – higher still – they climb the branches. Each robin tries to position itself above the other to show off their orange breast. Relentlessly, they chase each other from feeder to tree and back again like a feathered dogfight. If this fails to settle the score, they resort to outright fighting, sometimes to the death.

Such brutality often goes unseen in the British countryside at a glance, slipping behind a veil of prettiness, but that is the reality of it. I am watching one now, on an overcast November day, hopping in and out of the evergreen shrubs bordering the garden. It seems odd to relate such an inquisitive, seemingly peaceful, bird with violent rut-like encounters. Traditional English folk songs like 'The Robin' tend to agree, painting a scene of serenity.

The Robin
There came to my window one morning in spring
A sweet little robin, she came there to sing
The song that she sang, it was prettier far
Than any I've heard on a flute or guitar.

Her wings she was spreading to soar far away
Then resting a moment seemed sweetly to say
"Oh, happy, how happy the world seems to be
Awake, little girl, and be happy with me."

With both sexes having the same bright feathering on their breast, and their frequent garden visits, robins are instantly recognisable, like old friends. Unafraid to come closer than other birds might dare, it is as if a mutual trust extends between us.

Our propinquity with the robin is borne from their breeding and feeding behaviours.

Robins are not fussy nesters; all they require is a hole, which the female furnishes with moss, fallen leaves and grass. If left lying around, they will not think twice about cosying up in abandoned plant pots, boots, sheds and even kettles. Once, I heard about a green-fingered gentleman who hung his jacket over the fence on a warm spring day and returned to find a robin nesting in the pocket. No wonder folks call them the "gardener's friend"!

In fact, gardeners are very useful to the robin. Digging, folding, turning over and scuffing up gelid topsoil to uncover all of the invertebrate yumminess below. Robin watches on, perched idle on a spade or compost bag, waiting patiently for his meal to be served up on a soily platter – leaving the hard work to someone else. We are more than happy to help, a small gesture of thanks to the robin for brightening up our frosty winter days when other species migrate to warmer climes, chasing the sun.

\* \* \*

There are not nearly as many songs and rhymes (that we know of) relating to the robin as there are for the lark. Most famous of the known rhymes is 'Cock Robin', or 'Who Killed Cock Robin?', an English nursery rhyme first published in 1744. Although it was published in the eighteenth century, it is thought to be far older; the rhyming of "owl" with "shovel" in another version suggests a Middle English pronunciation, a form of English introduced after the 1066 Norman conquest and spoken until the late fifteenth century. The poem is lengthy, so I will include five verses, followed by the final verse.

## Robert Redbreast

Cock Robin
Who killed Cock Robin?
I, said the Sparrow,
with my bow and arrow,
I killed Cock Robin.

Who saw him die?
I, said the Fly,
with my little teeny eye,
I saw him die.

Who caught his blood?
I, said the Duck,
it was just my luck,
I caught his blood.

Who'll be the parson?
I, said the Rook,
with my little book,
I'll be the parson.

Who'll be the clerk?
I, said the Lark,
if it's not in the dark,
I'll be the clerk.

...

All the birds of the air
fell a-sighing and a-sobbing,
when they heard the bell toll
for poor Cock Robin.

There are many species mentioned in other verses: beetle, owl, linnet (a songbird included in very few folk songs), dove, kite, crow, thrush, wren and the bull – it's a long rhyme! Macabre as ever, there is an alternative ending where the sparrow held responsible for the death of Cock Robin is hanged.

A number of disputed theories have emerged to explain the dark folk narrative in this song, which describes the death and burial of the poor robin. The most convincing, I think, stems from Celtic pagan tradition. Lugh is a mythological sun god, who dies symbolically as the nights shorten after the summer solstice – he represents the red sun or *Coch Rhi Ben* in Welsh, anglicised to "Cock Robin". The murderous sparrow who kills the robin with a bow and arrow is said to represent Brân the Blessed, a god of winter, even though Brân is usually translated from Welsh as 'crow' or 'raven'. Such allegorical interpretations transform the rhyme into a seasonal battle in which winter triumphs over summer, as it does each year. With the summer sun defeated, no wonder "all the birds of the air" are so remorseful. They ought to be reassured that spring will come, and new life with it.

'Cock Robin' was published in *Tommy Thumb's Pretty Song-Book* (1744) – a sequel to the earliest known collection of English nursery rhymes, which is tragically lost. Nestled within the pages are some of the oldest printed texts of many well-loved traditional children's songs, including 'Baa Baa Black Sheep' and 'Hickory Dickory Dock'. Even if the original authors were known, it is hard to imagine anyone creating these timeless classics. They seem undatable, like they have always been there. We do not learn them; we just know them. Makeshift dances and pat-a-cake style clapping games swirl up to accompany the rhymes on playgrounds across the country.

# Robert Redbreast

This songbook is of note here because the robin stars in not just one rhyme, 'Cock Robin', but a second in the form 'Little Robin Redbreast'. Its prominence within this foundational collection is astounding – a true testament to just how long ago the robin befriended us.

While 'Little Robin Redbreast' varies from source to source, the following two variants are the most common. The first is a "fingerplay", meaning that you can act out the scene with your own digits. I will put these (admittedly vague) instructions in brackets, which were first included in a version from 1920 – have a go as you read:

Little Robin Redbreast
Little Robin Redbreast
Sat upon a rail;
*(Right hand extended in shape of a bird is poised on extended forefinger of left hand)*
Niddle noddle went his head,
And waggle went his tail.
*(Little finger of right hand waggles from side to side)*

Little Robin Redbreast
Came to visit me;
This is what he whistled:
"Thank you for my tea."

The second variant, my favourite of the two, has no such finger display:

Little Robin Redbreast sat upon a tree,
Up went the Pussy-Cat and down went he;
Down came Pussy-Cat away Robin ran,
Says Little Robin Redbreast – "Catch me if you can".

# Singing Like Larks

Little Robin Redbreast jumped upon a wall,
Pussy-Cat jumped after him, and almost got a fall.
Little Robin chirped and sung, and what did pussy say?
Pussy-Cat said, "Meow, Meow, Meow" – and Robin jumped
away.

\* \* \*

We have already encountered the robin-wren alliance in this book. The marriage between the "tame ruddock", as Chaucer put it, and the tiny wren has been played out multiple times in literature, and they have represented husband and wife since at least 1400. Robert Burns imagined 'The Marriage of Robin Redbreast and the Wren' in the eighteenth century when he was just a teenager, describing how the feathered pair came into their love bond. Isabella Begg, Burns' youngest sister, recalled in her eighties that Robert wrote a festive piece about it to entertain his younger siblings. It is not a song nor poem, but an enchanting fairy tale written in thick Scottish dialect, with the proper title reading 'Robin Reidbreist and the Wran'. Paraphrasing Burns' story, we read:

*Early one morning, an old grey cat called Poussie Baudrons came across Robin Redbreast sitting by the water-side and said, "Where are you going, wee Robin?"*

*He replied, "I'm on my way to sing a song to the King on this fine Yule morning." The cat beckoned Robin closer saying, "Come and look at this ring of white fur around my neck."*

*"No!" snapped Robin, "You might worry the wee mouse, but you don't worry me."*

*Robin flew away and landed upon the fence of a sheepfold,*

where he saw a greedy grey hawk stretching its wings. The hawk said, "Where are you going, wee robin?" The robin repeated his words to the cat, explaining that he was off to sing a Yuletide song to the King. "Come here, wee Robin, and see this bonny feather in my wing," said the hawk. Robin saw through this folly saying, "No! You may have plucked a wee linnet, but you won't pluck me."

Again Robin flew, this time until he came to a gorge where he spied a fox called Tod Lowrie sitting on the craig. "Where are you going, wee Robin?" said the fox. Once again Robin explained his quest. Tod Lowrie replied, "Come here, wee Robin, and I'll show you the spot on my tail." Robin was wise to this and, unwilling to become the fox's lunch, replied, "No! You may have savaged the lamb, but you won't savage me."

Finally, Robin came to a bonny burn-side where he saw a boy sitting. The same conversation unfolded until the boy said, "Come here, wee Robin, and I'll give you some crumbs from my pouch." Bravely, Robin denied once more, "No! You may have torn the goldfinch apart, but you'll not tear me."

Away he flew once more until he came before the King. There he sat on the windowsill and sang his Yuletide song, to which the King said to the Queen: "What shall we give to wee Robin for singing us this bonny song?" The Queen replied, "I think we'll give him wee Wren to be his wife." So it came to be that the Robin and Wren were married, and the King, Queen and all the court danced freely before the new-lyweds returned to Robin's waterside and sat upon a brier.

In the repeated question, "Where are you going, wee Robin?" I hear the echo of "What's the time, Mr Wolf?" from the timeless childhood game, and even "Where are you going to, little brown mouse?" from Julia Donaldson's *The Gruffalo* (1999). Written with the same structure, it is evident that Burns' story stems from the same corner of fairy-tale tradition, full of memorable hooks that keep us reading and sharing again and again.

\* \* \*

"Ruddock" was the robin's first name in England, dating back as early as 600 A.D. and said to be derived from the Old English "ræd" or Latin "*ruber*", both meaning "red". Robins are ruddy birds, although this description seems impolite nowadays. Simply called the "redbreast" for centuries, their proximity to humans earnt them the familiar sobriquet "Robert" around the sixteenth century, eventually forming the alliterative "Robert Redbreast". This was shortened to the hypocoristic "Robin", which is how the species has been referred to ever since.

The names "Robert" and "Robin" caught on, yet he seemed incomplete without a hen beside him. All of the small birds were eligible for a time, but only the wren possessed the required charms, as well as a pleasingly neat rhyme with "hen". Jenny Wren became the bride-to-be. Exactly why these two love birds were joined together, we will never fully know.

Is Robin "Orangebreast" a more accurate name than "Redbreast"? Looking at them objectively, their breast is clearly orange, not red. However, there is a good reason why the colour orange was not used to originally describe the robin. "Ruddock" and "Redbreast" were in use before the fifteenth century, but the orange (and subsequently the citrus colour bearing the same name) was not unloaded onto Britain's shores until the sixteenth century. The word simply did not exist here yet! Before oranges came to town, things that bore this colour were simply called "yellow-red" or just "red".

Many tales explain how the robin acquired its ruddy, fiery breast. Christian folklore transports us to Jesus' stable when he was born, where a robin tries to help out the wren, singeing his feathers in the process:

*Long ago, the wren stole fire from the heavens and returned to earth entirely aflame. Birds queued up to donate their spare feathers, helping the wren to replace the ones that she had lost. The robin was most anxious of them all, straying too close to the burning wren and getting scorched in the process, reddening his belly for evermore.*

\* \* \*

Before the existence of genetic analysis, the robin was classified into the thrush family (*Turdidae*) because of behavioural similarities. Standing boldly upright like a robin, the mistle thrush has a black-spotted breast reminiscent of ermine fur lining a coronation robe and crown. Like thrushes, the robin sings loudly, and all of them skulk in the undergrowth for food. The similarities go on and on.

More in-depth analysis, however, reveals that the robin actually belongs to the *Muscicapidae* family – the Old World flycatchers. "Old World" refers to the parts of the world known before contact with the Americas – Europe, Africa and Asia – although it sounds like a term from *The Hobbit*. These flycatchers are true to their name, feeding on insects they catch on the wing; flyfishing for their bait, which is a mixture of beetles, mealworms and other bugs, seizing them from grass and sorrel tips.

Still, this misclassification is preserved in 'Robin-a-Thrush', a song found in Europe and America. The lines in italics are repeated in each verse.

# Singing Like Larks

Robin-a-Thrush
Oh, Robin-a-Thrush he married a wife,
*With a hoppity-moppity moan-oh.*
She proved to be the plague of his life,
*With a hig jig jiggety, ruffety petticoat,*
*Robin-a-Thrush cries moan-oh!*

And she never got up till twelve o' clock,
She put on a gown and never a smock.

She milked the cow just once a week,
She said it made the butter taste sweet.

Her cheese when made was put on the shelf,
And it never got turned till it turned of itself.

Well it turned and turned till it walked on the floor,
It stood upon legs and walked to the door.

It walked till it came to Banbury Fair,
The dame followed after upon a grey mare.

This song it was made for gentlemen,
If you want any more you must sing it again.

Comedic songs about slothful wives, like this one, have been common since the Middle Ages, especially in northern England, although I fear they have not aged well!

\* \* \*

It is time to address the reindeer in the room – Christmas – the day that comes to mind every time I see a robin. A time of year when my mind settles, and magic permeates the gaps vacated by the stress of everyday life. Transcending daily routines, reflection takes over during the festive season and each year I am reminded of the joy that spending time with family, thoughtful gift giving and nature's downtime can bring.

Walking around the block to gather my thoughts, the first Christmas lights have shown themselves, dug out from dusty lofts to breathe through the darkest nights. Red, green, golden and flashing white bulbs adorn the homes of festive souls, proclaiming to passers-by in December, "You are not alone." Traffic noise turns to silence and, returning to my front door I am hit by a lovely warmth as I open it. Just before I shut it behind me a lone robin sings through the inky blackness from a telegraph pole, half-lit by glowing Christmas cheer.

Even the sight of a robin in the height of summer transports me deep into the heart of an icy winter, walking through powdery snow, making that satisfying crumple sound underfoot. It reminds me of the big day in December, and everything that comes with it; I shall refrain from describing the workshop, the miniature sleigh or eight tiny "you know whats" in order to contain the phrenetic child within. Watching over all of the seasonal festivities with an observant beady eye is always the robin – a splash of colour on winter's greyscale canvas – picking red berries from the prickly bush that bears the crown.

> Oh, the holly and the ivy
> When they are both full grown;
> Of all the trees that are in the wood
> The holly bears the crown.[7]

So, how did robins become associated with Christmas in the first place? It supposedly began with the "penny post" in 1840 and the decades following that when exchanging Christmas cards took off commercially. At the time, postmen in Victorian Britain wore bright red tunics resembling the bird and so were called "Robins". As we know, postmen deliver Christmas cards and, as cards were being created featuring robins dressed up in the postman's uniform, it was not long before they were depicted clutching Yuletide messages in their beaks. Such images certainly give fresh meaning to a round-robin letter!

This postal portrayal of the robin grafted neatly onto their traditional folkloric role as winged messengers for the spirit world. Sticking close by and singing, it does feel like they are trying to tell us something, trying to deliver a message. To this day, many take comfort from their presence not just at Christmastime, but all year round – after all, "when robins appear, loved ones are near".

The robin has always been my Yuletide messenger. I was told as a child that robins are Father Christmas's personal helpers, watching each child diligently throughout the year and reporting back to the big man himself, holding great sway in one of the most important decisions in a child's year: naughty or nice? Even now, when a robin is close, I'm on my best behaviour – take no chances! After writing my yearly letter to Father Christmas and carefully decorating it, I would peg it onto the branch of a small leafless tree in my garden and leave it overnight to be collected by the robins, ready to be flown to the North Pole. It was always gone by morning.

\* \* \*

The next traditional ballad, 'Babes in the Wood', is not a cheerful account. The lyrics are hundreds of years old, but stem from an even older folk tale. Like many ancient stories, there is a warning at its core, with the title becoming a widespread expression referring to an innocent person entering unawares into a potentially dangerous situation. In short, the *Hansel and Gretel*-like narrative is the story of two young orphans whose callous uncle pays two men to take them into a Norfolk wood and kill them in an attempt to claim their fortune. Unable to go through with it, the criminals abandon the children, who wander alone in the wood and, unable to fend for themselves, eventually succumb to the elements. They are reclaimed by the earth and covered with leaves by robins (and a wren in some versions).

Ballads were written to relate this tale and it was even adapted for film by Walt Disney in 1932. Here are five verses from 'The Babes in the Wood', a ballad published by Thomas Millington in 1595:

Now ponder well, you parents dear,
These words which I shall write;
A doleful story you shall hear,
In time brought forth to light.
A gentleman of good account
In Norfolk dwelt of late.
Who did in honour far surmount
Most men of his estate.

"Now, brother," said the dying man,
"Look to my children dear;
Be good unto my boy and girl,
No friends else have they here:
"To God and you I do commend
My children dear this day;
But little while be sure we have
Within this world to stay."

The parents being dead and gone,
The children home he takes,
And brings them straight unto his house,
Where much of them he makes.
He had not kept these pretty babes
A twelvemonth and a day,
But, for their wealth, he did devise
To make them both away.

He bargain'd with two ruffians strong,
Which were of furious mood,
That they should take the children young,
And slay them in a wood.
He told his wife an artful tale,
He would the children send
To be brought up in faire London,
With one that was his friend.

Thus wandered these two pretty babes,
Till death did end their grief;
In one another's arms they dyed,
As babes wanting relief.
No burial these pretty babes
Of any man receives,
Till Robin-Redbreast piously
Did cover them with leaves.

The "pious" robin paints this species as devoutly religious, like an angel comforting the innocent children as they transition to the next world. Such imagery connects to a whole host of ancient Christian stories, some of which we have already seen, like the robin's presence at Jesus's stable when he was born. As well as 'The Babes in the Wood', the robin is said to have played a similar comforting role at Christ's crucifixion, covering him with leaves and permanently staining his breast feathers red with blood. Coming to represent both the summer and the winter – light and dark, beginning and end, life and death, alpha and omega – it is fitting that the robin is described as having been present at Christ's birth and death.

As Bob Copper reflects in *A Song for Every Season* (1971), the following version of 'Babes in the Wood' has been etched into the Copper Family's Christmas tradition for centuries:

Babes in the Wood
O, don't you remember a long time ago
Those two little babies their names I don't know,
They strayed away one bright summer's day,
Those two little babies got lost on their way.

*Chorus (repeated after each verse):*
Pretty babes in the wood, pretty babes in the wood,
O, don't you remember those babes in the wood?

Now the day being done and the night coming on
Those two little babies sat under a stone.
They sobbed and they sighed they sat there and cried,
Those two little babies they lay down and died.

Now the robins so red how swiftly they sped,
They put out their wide wings and over them spread.
And all the day long in the branches they throng,
They sweetly did whistle and this was their song.

Bob remembered Christmas as a boy in Rottingdean, in the early 1920s. The brittle air lay over thin soils and the flint poked through like a winter crop. Harvest was long since over and the shortest December days were livened with flocks of cawing sea birds, driven inland in search of food by channel gales. Hand bell ringing and practice for the yearly Mummer's Play had been going on for a fortnight down at The Black Horse but, when the twenty-fifth rolled around, the Coppers would always gather in Brasser's little terraced cottage – Bob's grandfather and foreman of the farm.

Star-leafed ivy decorated the dresser and sprigs of holly festooned the mantle. Trestle tables creaked beneath the weight of food and drink, especially the turkey which had to be cooked in the local baker's oven on Christmas morning – so enormous that you "could cut an' come ag'in," as Bob put it. Casks of Christmas ale and double stout, tucked away all year, made an appearance early on in the proceedings but, for all its festivities, Christmas Day came with one strict rule: no wines or spirits on the table before 9:30 p.m.

After a hearty roast, attention soon moved from the table to the fireside, where Brasser, seated in an armchair, would give the reverential nod and all would launch into the first carol. Blood harmonies raised the roof, and the conflation of worshipping voices fairly shook the walls. Passers-by would pause in the street and listen, pleased to hear the family keeping up their annual tradition.

Only when the sacred Christmas carols and hymns had been exhausted would the old "Copper songs" follow. By supper at 11 p.m. they were still hard at it, digging into ham and a cold rabbit pie thick with jelly. As one side of the room wrestled with a forkful, the other half of the room would strike up two lines of 'Babes in the Wood', and as the singing side took a bite from their plate, the other half quickly swallowed their mouthfuls and continued the verse. Then everyone had to clear their mouths in time to join in with the chorus! Verses swung back and forth across the fire like a game of tennis, simultaneously maintaining both song and supper, and this remarkable polyphony continued until Boxing Day arrived.

The robin was present inside and out: sweetly singing from the bare branches outside the flinty walls of their cottage and found proudly within the lyrics, which are still sung by the family today.

\* \* \*

Appearing in folk songs of quality, not quantity, scarcely one bad word is sung about the robin: winged messengers, Santa's little helpers, holy and god-fearing spirits. Colouring our winters with warm tones and providing comfort when we need it most, these special birds are rightly celebrated in song and verse for their loyal and enduring friendship with humans – we love them for it. Oh, yes, the average robin may only live for thirteen months, but as my twin brother Tom once said, "At least they get a Christmas."

A little robin sweetly singing
Came to my window on a Christmas day
And from his little throat came ringing
A most melodious lay.

'The Robin's Christmas Carol', The Leisure Hour (1896)

# Yon Little Turtle Dove

## (*Streptopelia turtur*)

*O don't you see yon little turtle dove,*
*Sitting under the mulberry tree?*

– 'The Little Turtle Dove'

THE TURTLE DOVE IS SUMMER ITSELF. Arriving in late April from the dusty African Sahel – the broad line between the tropics and desert – this shy, watchful bird seemingly carries the heat on its wings. More widely travelled than most, their scaly tortoiseshell plumage, blue-lagoon colouration and exotic pink eye rings showcase their worldliness, setting them apart from their closest UK relative, the paler collared dove which is a bold coloniser from the East.

Collared doves call out the familiar "hoo hoooo-hoo" but are outclassed by the turtle dove's soporific "turrr turrr turr", bassy enough to cleave bark from trees and cover orchard floors with freshly fallen fruit – or so it seems. Such a full-throated, rolling song is the reason behind the second part of this species' taxonomic name – *turtur*.

# *Yon Little Turtle Dove*

As I write this, a gang of dalmatian-like doves and pigeons (although none of a turtle persuasion) are sitting in a row and peering down at me from the flat roof at the end of the garden. Pure white release doves are rumoured to have been set free during the opening of the nearby London 2012 Olympic bike track, and they went on to breed with others from the *Columbidae* family (chiefly local woodpigeons, stock and collared doves) creating many pigeon-dove hybrids who look as if they have all been splashed with white paint. This bizarre group of pied birds all live harmoniously under a large roof solar panel, sheltered from the elements and predators. On one particularly bright spring day, one of them max-relaxed in a dog's metal water bowl at the end of a driveway which had been warmed by the sun – it looked like a dove spa day.

Anyway, Victorians recount seeing flocks of flying turtle doves. But, on my patch, not one graces the sky.

\* \* \*

Turtle doves are celebrated for one reason in particular – they mate for life. This is true of many dove species, which form enduring pair bonds until the end. Working collaboratively to raise a brood, the female will incubate a clutch of two milk-white eggs during the day, swapping at dusk with the male. Their loyal and selfless sharing of familial responsibility is admired, explaining why they are often depicted and released at weddings as a symbol of lifelong devotion. Since early Greek and Roman civilisations, the groom has traditionally gifted a dove to his bride – a promise to care for her and her family.

In the Old Testament, Noah sends out a dove from his ark to find land during the Great Flood. It returns with an olive leaf in its beak, a sign that the waters have subsided. For this deed, the dove has come to symbolise the Holy Spirit, set in stained glass and embroidered onto priests' vestments as the essence of peace, renewal and forgiveness. Such heavenly depictions flow through the folk tradition, with the generic dove (potentially representing over 300 species) used to represent true love and, more often than not, the loss of it.

Dink's Song
If I had wings, like Noah's dove,
I'd fly up the river to the one I love.
*Fare thee well, oh honey, fare thee well. (Refrain)*

Early one morning, drizzling rain,
And in my heart, I felt an aching pain.

I had a man, an' he's long and tall,
He moves his body like a cannonball.

One of these mornings, it won't be long,
You'll call my name and I'll be gone.

Dink was the name of an African American woman from whom this song was collected in 1909. First published by collector John Lomax in an anthology called *American Ballads and Folk Songs* (1934), the story goes that as he was strolling along the Brazos River in Texas, he spotted a woman beside a levee under construction, quietly singing the blues. She was busy washing her husband's clothes in the shade of a tent camp of migratory builders.

Dink stopped singing when Lomax approached. Each time he asked her to sing she would reply, "Today ain't my singin' day." A bottle of gin bought at a local commissary store was shared between them, and she eventually warmed to him, singing this mournful song about a woman deserted by her man. The original tune is lost, with old recordings broken long ago. As Lomax puts it, "What is left is only a shadow of the tender, tragic beauty of what she sang in the sordid, bleak surroundings of a Brazos Bottom levee camp".

To envy a bird's freedom in flight is indeed a "tender, tragic" thought, well captured in the song. The loneliness felt after being parted from someone we love might be eased if only we too had wings to fly back to them, just as a turtle dove can fly back to its nest.

Marcus Mumford, of the band Mumford & Sons, sang a revamped version of 'Dink's Song' with Hollywood actor Oscar Isaac for the 2013 film *Inside Llewyn Davis*, directed by the Coen Brothers. The film follows a week in the life of Llewyn Davis, a former merchant marine and fictional composite of real-life American folk singer Dave Van Ronk (1936–2002). It is set in New York City's Greenwich Village during the 1960s folk revival.

Despite Llewyn's talent, his records are not selling. His singing partner has died, he has no money, no home – not even a winter coat. With his romantic relationship in tatters, Llewyn appears fed up with life – condemned to return to sea as a fisherman – his love of folk music is simply not enough to sustain him. Isaac's incredible acting makes it hard to watch Llewyn's desperation and longing for freedom, travelling from one dead end to the next, which makes his performance of 'Dink's Song' so heart-wrenching. If only he could fly away like Noah's dove; maybe then he might be missed, and his work finally appreciated.

# Singing Like Larks

Most of the film soundtrack is comprised of songs from Van Ronk's repertoire – including 'Dink's Song' – and his fifth studio album, *Inside Dave Van Ronk*, has an almost identical cover to Llewyn's album in the film: tweed jacket, leaning against a doorway, cigarette in hand.

The movie paints a pitiless picture of life in the Village at this time in history, especially the clutching, impoverished despair self-inflicted in the pursuit of art. Smoky folk clubs like the Gaslight Café were called "basket houses" because performers would pass around a basket at the end of each set, hoping to receive some form of payment, and musical instruments were lumbered between venues in all weathers as musicians tried desperately to get noticed by a record label.

It seems that no matter how good you were, it was all right place, right time, right song. Some made it, others did not. 'Dink's Song' and many others became staples for folk singers during this revival, as they mined the past for the uncontrived authenticity found in old ballads. Defining a folk song is difficult, but Llewyn comes close just before playing the song with this throwaway line: "You've probably heard this one before. If it was never new, and it never gets old, then it's a folk song."

The Gaslight Café, now closed, was a coffeehouse on MacDougal Street in Greenwich Village and was one of the first places Bob Dylan played publicly, later releasing an album called *Live at The Gaslight 1962*. It sculpted some of the eras most famous talents, like Hendrix and Springsteen, who all climbed down the steep stairs that led to this jazz, poetry and folk-heavy basement bar. Dave Van Ronk was such a regular that he became known as the "mayor of MacDougal Street". Today the café is a cocktail bar; the appetite for folk music has wavered.

The version of 'Dink's Song' that Mumford sings in the film circles back around to birds at the end: "Just as sure as a bird flying high above / Life ain't worth living, without the one you love". If any species knows this to be true, it is the turtle dove. They have been known to watch over a deceased mate for some time, even returning to the place where they died after the body is gone. Only after this period of apparent mourning will they move on and find a new mate. Some never do.

\* \* \*

Choosing to book their summer holidays to the UK, turtle doves often represent this season in songs – even in the biblical 'Song of Songs', otherwise known as the 'The Song of Solomon':

*For lo, the winter is past, the rain is over and gone. The flowers appear on the earth; the time of the singing birds is come, and the voice of the turtle is heard in our land.*

Later versions of this Bible verse alter "turtle" to "turtle dove", for clarity's sake, tactfully dodging images of singing aquatic reptiles.

The seasonality of the turtle dove certainly did not go over the heads of rural folk singers. Cast your mind back to 'Sweet Lemeney', filled with nightingales and larks.

*As I was a-walking one fine summer's morning…*

…

*On yonder green bower the turtle doves are building…*

A fitting inclusion for a summertime song concerning two young lovers, and their sad parting. However, it is not just the warm season that they represent – every time there is trouble in love, the turtle dove seemingly makes an appearance.

This is true of 'The Deserted Dairymaid', which I found in an obscure little sage green songbook published in 1979 called *Bushes & Briars: An Anthology of Essex Folk Songs*, compiled by D. Occomore and P. Spratley. It is stapled together and faded. Before this collection, virtually nothing had been written on the folk songs of Essex which, due to this county's geographical position, were greatly influenced by the broadside ballads being mass produced in London throughout the seventeenth, eighteenth and nineteenth centuries. Essex farmers and carriers travelling up to city markets often brought home a street ballad to amuse their friends. Conversely, ballad printers were always on the lookout for a good song sung by an Essex countryman coming up to the London fairs and markets.

All that is known of this sea song, included in the book without a melody, is that it was "collected from Mr Dan'l Francis".

The Deserted Dairymaid
As I walked out one fine morning
One midsummer morning so early,
I found a fair maid by my way,
I says, 'Are you young Mary?'

I asked where she was a-going,
This midsummer morning so early,
'I'm going a-milking, sir' she cried
'And then going in my dairy'.

I says, 'My dear, pray go with me,
Forsake your cows and dairy,
For I will make a captain's bride

Of my charming blue-eyed Mary'.

Down on the mossy bank we sat,
I was sure there was no other near me,
And then I kissed the rubond lips
Of my charming blue-eyed Mary.

I gave to her a diamond ring,
One midsummer morning early,
Once more I kissed the rubond lips
Of my charming blue-eyed Mary.

And then I says 'I must away
My ship, it sails so early,
I'll prove as true as turtle dove,
To you my blue-eyed Mary'.

When six long months were gone and passed
No letter came to Mary
She often viewed her diamond ring
When she was in her dairy.

\* \* \*

Neat, dainty and dapper, one might expect this chestnut-and-black-patterned bird to have a stylish nest to match – the equivalent of some five-bed townhouse made with the sturdiest of twigs and fitted with a state-of-the-art seed dispenser whilst the turtle dove itself organises hedge funds from within the hedgerow. In all seriousness, their nests are surprisingly flimsy and slapdash, placed within a tall bower of hawthorn, elder or other thorny shrub, messily thrown together with twigs, plant stalks and soft grass to line the bottom.

The following clump of familial turtle dove songs resembles

their messy nest – difficult to piece together. All of them are the same song at heart but have diverged to such a degree that they feel completely separate from one another.

Let's begin with 'The Turtle Dove', also called 'Ten Thousand Miles'. In 1903, Vaughan Williams rode his bicycle past the Plough, an ancient oak-beamed pub in Rusper, West Sussex. He decided to pop in, asking: "Anyone know any songs?" The landlord sang this to him, which he had never heard before. Vaughan Williams took it away to London and made it a global hit. His arrangement has been recorded time and time again – my favourite is Peter Bellamy's version, free to listen to on YouTube. Sadly, in the song, the delicate wild dove mourns for its own isolation and disappearance.

The Turtle Dove
Oh don't you see yon little turtle dove
Sitting under the mulberry tree
And a-making mourn for his own true love
As I shall mourn for thee, my dear,
As I shall mourn for thee.

So you must suffer grief and pain,
'Tis but for a little while.
And wherever I will go I will return,
Though I go ten thousand mile, my dear,
Though I go ten thousand mile.

Ten thousand mile it is too far
To leave me all alone,
While I must lie, lament and cry,
And you'll not hear my moan, my dear,
And you'll not hear my moan.

# Yon Little Turtle Dove

Well the tide it shall seize to beat the shore
And stars shall fall from the sky,
Yet I will love thee more and more,
Until the day I die, my dear,
Until the day I die.

Then let the seas run dry, my dear,
And rocks all melt in the sun,
Yet here I'll stay and never from thee part,
Till all these things be done, my dear,
Till all these things be done.

Oh don't you see yon little turtle dove
Sitting under the mulberry tree
A-making mourn for his own true love
As I shall mourn for thee, my dear,
As I shall mourn for thee.

Song collector A.L. Lloyd commented in the linear notes of his 1956 album, *The Foggy Dew and Other Traditional English Love Songs*, that, around 1770, leaflets containing these lyrics were being hawked about fairgrounds in England and Scotland. Milkmaids and horse handlers would stick them to the walls of "dairy and stable" to learn the songs while they worked. Robert Burns is rumoured to have obtained one of these turtle dove handouts, which became a driving inspiration for his song 'A Red, Red Rose' (1794), which shares almost identical lines:

Till a' the seas gang dry, my dear,
And the rocks melt wi' the sun;
I will love thee still, my dear
While the sands o' life shall run.

And fare thee weel, my only luve!

And fare thee weel awhile!
And I will come again, my luve,
Though it were ten thousand mile.

'The Little Turtle Dove' is another song which begins exactly as 'The Turtle Dove' does, being as closely related as their names suggest, but this one includes alternative verses:

The crow that's black, my little turtle dove,
Shall change its colour white;
Before I'm false to the maiden I love,
The noon-day shall be night, my dear,
The noon-day shall be night.

The hills shall fly, my little turtle dove,
The roaring billows burn,
Before my heart shall suffer me to fail,
Or I a traitor turn, my dear,
Or I a traitor turn.

To add another layer of complexity to this musical jigsaw, both 'The Turtle Dove' and 'The Little Turtle Dove' are thought to be later variants of a song called 'The True Lover's Farewell'. First published in 1710, Cecil Sharp (1859-1924) collected nine of its variants. Sharp was a co-founder of the English Folk Dance Society, which later merged into the English Folk Dance and Song Society (EFDSS) – the hub of folk music in England today.

Joan Baez, a matriarch of American folk music, sings a variant called 'Fare Thee Well'. Baez, originally from New York, broke through during the 1960s Greenwich Village folk scene and has performed for over sixty years. She performed all around the circuit at the same time as John Denver, Joni

Mitchell, Pete Seeger and Bob Dylan and at hootenannies[8] in clubs and coffeehouses like The Bitter End in New York, which is still open today.

I will never forget when first I heard Baez's high-pitched, hauntingly clear voice. I was listening to her recording of the chilling sixteenth-century Scottish ballad 'Mary Hamilton', about "the four Marys" who were ladies in waiting to Mary Queen of Scots. Instant goosebumps. To this day, she takes little credit for her ability to strip a song back to its roots, guiding the listener to a sullen wedding night on the streets of Glasgow half a millennia ago or, in the case of 'Fare Thee Well', to the parting of lovers now both forgotten, whilst the turtle dove gazes on. Baez best summarises her abilities in the opening line of her memoir, *And a Voice to Sing With*: "I was born gifted."

'Fare Thee Well' retells this romantic separation in a slightly different way to its musical cousins, leaving out the turtle dove altogether. Cropping up in most songs featuring turtle doves, the phrase "fare thee well" is found in countless English ballads dating back to at least the eighteenth century. It is an example of a "floating line" (although to call it a "flying line" would be more satisfying). This is when a line, or an entire verse, is reused and recycled in multiple songs, almost allowing folk songs to stay connected and talk to one another as they adapt and change through time. This one begins:

Fare you well my dear, I must be gone
And leave you for a while
If I roam away I'll come back again
Though I roam ten thousand miles, my dear
Though I roam ten thousand miles.

# Singing Like Larks

This family of songs encapsulate the evolving musical tradition. Verses are altered or omitted (purposefully or not) over time to the tune of each singer's will and individual taste, and new ones put in. The result? A melting pot of creativity, and enough turtle dove lyrics to fill the pages of a songbook.

\* \* \*

Not all turtle dove songs are so mournful. Belfast-born Freddy McKay (1914–97) was a witty and comedic man, and singer Peta Webb recalls how he was remarkably principled, living life according to: "stand up, speak out, shut up, sit down". He performed at folk clubs like The Fox, Islington Green, for decades and it was once said that a good folk club was "one Freddy McKay goes to". He wrote the comic parody song 'Silver Dagger, Turtle Dove', which contrasts with his own integrous character, as an unheroic rake proudly recounts his two-timing ways in the opening verse:

> In Liverpool town where I did dwell,
> There was a maid I loved right well,
> But I loved a lot of others too,
> And to this maid I proved untrue.

> *Chorus:*
> With me ding dong derroll silver dagger,
> Ding dong derroll turtle dove.

It is an odd song. The maid tries to kill herself by sticking her head in the oven and, finding there is no gas, hangs herself instead. When her father cuts her down she falls on top of the undertaker and kills him too. The mother walks in to see her fallen on top of him and cries, "At last my daughter's got a man!" and calls for a turtle dove to be sent as a sign of their bond. The song's strangeness draws me in because, despite being written in the 1970s, the population decline of this bird was clearly already being felt in the UK – illustrated in the lines that follow the mother's request:

But turtle doves are scarce and few,
A budgerigar will have to do.

McKay always encouraged people to share and learn his songs as if they were traditional, so I hope he would be pleased that these lines are included here.

\* \* \*

The title of the next song hints at its subject matter – drink. 'There is a Tavern in the Town' first appeared in an 1883 anthology called *Student Songs* and is sung to a similar tune as 'Heads, Shoulders, Knees and Toes'. Drinking songs are a global affair, called "*trinklieder*" in Germany and "*dryckesvisor*" in Sweden, with some traceable back to the eleventh century. Nothing breaks down walls like a song, and booze is certainly conducive to a singaround.

There is a Tavern in the Town
There is a tavern in the town, in the town
And there my true love sits him down, sits him down,
And drinks his wine as merry as can be,
And never, never thinks of me.

*Chorus:*
Fare thee well, for I must leave thee,
Do not let this parting grieve thee,

# Singing Like Larks

And remember that the best of friends
Must part, must part.

Adieu, adieu kind friends, adieu, adieu, adieu,
I can no longer stay with you, stay with you,
I will hang my harp on the weeping willow tree,
And may the world go well with thee.

He left me for a damsel dark, damsel dark,
Each Friday night they used to spark, used to spark,
And now my love who once was true to me
Takes this dark damsel on his knee.

And now I see him nevermore, nevermore;
He never knocks upon my door, on my door;
Oh, woe is me; he pinned a little note,
And these were all the words he wrote:

Oh, dig my grave both wide and deep, wide and deep;
Put tombstones at my head and feet, head and feet
And on my breast you may carve a turtle dove,
To signify I died of love.

The symbolism of the turtle dove is laid out explicitly in the final verse – a sign of unfaltering, devoted love, carved permanently onto the heart. A closely related song called 'The Bold Young Farmer', collected in 1904 from Nevinton, Essex, includes an almost identical final verse, but the preceding verses are quite different. Sung from the perspective of a young girl, she sadly explains how a farmer courted her, before leaving her for a richer woman:

It's grief to me, I'll tell you why,
Because she has more gold than I,

But in needy time her gold shall fly,
And she shall be as poor as I.

There is a bird in yonder tree,
They say it's blind and cannot see,
I wish it had been the same with me,
Before I joined his company.

Bing Crosby and Nat King Cole performed 'There is a Tavern in the Town', their voices bringing to mind images of a white Christmas and chestnuts roasting on an open fire. It is well-known that the turtle dove, despite being a summer visitor, has its own links to the festive season. As the feathered figure-head for love, sharing and tenderness, the turtle dove makes an appearance in perhaps the most famous Yuletide carol of all, 'The Twelve Days of Christmas'.

On the second day of Christmas, my true love sent to me,
Two turtle doves and a partridge in a pear tree.

First published in England in 1780 as a children's memorisation game, although thought to be of French origin, in the song the turtle dove is accompanied by seven swans-a-swimming, four colly birds, three French hens, and a partridge in a pear tree – despite being a ground-dwelling bird.

The song cares little for ornithological fact but does the turtle dove justice by gifting two together, and not just for the sake of alliteration. Once again, birds step in to plug the gaps where our own wordy descriptions fall short: warm connections in the icy depths of winter – two birds and two humans unbreakable in their attachments. The present speaks for itself.

\* \* \*

# Singing Like Larks

When I started writing this chapter, it dawned on me that I had never seen a turtle dove. They pop up in traditional songs like the common birds they once were, but their purring sound of the summer is now unfamiliar.

Droughts in their African wintering grounds and the loss of the outstretched acacia trees in which they roost are making life difficult for them. Their welcome here is no better, with the cutting back and removal of hedges used to nest and the use of herbicides killing the weeds whose seeds they rely on for food. As UK populations fail to breed, fewer birds return to traditional breeding sites the following year and the downward spiral continues. Thankfully, "Operation Turtle Dove", a partnership of RSPB, Natural England, Pensthorpe Conservation Trust and Fair to Nature, are working directly with forward-thinking farmers to bring this emblematic species back from the brink, leaving unsprayed margins on their fields which allow wild lowland flowering plants like purply-pink fumitory – the smoke of the earth – to shoot up, providing a food source for the turtle doves until they migrate south for the winter.

It is not just the ecological threats in their respective breeding sites that threaten the population, but the actual migration itself. A fierce ballad could be written about the deadly challenge the turtle doves face as they run the gauntlet to and from Europe during their spring and autumn migration. As they fly in a straight line across southern Mediterranean nations – *Crack!* – they are shot out of the skies. Malta, Italy, France and many other European countries have allowed millions of this species to be massacred for decades – once for food, now seemingly for fun. If it were to stop, the European population would begin to bounce back almost immediately. Yes, turtle doves need breeding grounds, ponds and a reliable food source in this country, but populations will never recover if they are shot en route.

Such a neglection of our own role as stewards sees our summertime symbol of love replaced with a screaming absence in sky and hedgerow. It's part of a wider silencing of Britain's wild spaces. For every hundred turtle doves in our countryside half a century ago, there are now just two. Emboldened by the turtle dove songs in this chapter, I woke up one Thursday in May and set out on a mission with the express intention of seeing a turtle dove in the UK.

Heading against the early morning traffic, I drove north into the countryside. Shades on. Windows down. The roads became gradually smaller until I reached an empty single-lane track leading into Essex Wildlife Trust's Fingringhoe Wick Nature Reserve, where I had seen nightingales not long before. Walking past the red-brick visitor centre and onto the gravel paths, the lofty hedges grew well above head height, quilted with white hawthorn, fruitless brambles and yellow gorse flowers.

Rounding each corner, I seemed to be breaking up secretive meetings of stately pheasants, blackbirds, rabbits and other wildlife which either flew away or road-runnered off into the thicket at my presence. A brimstone butterfly held its lime-green paper wings to the light, showing off every vein. My ears were wide open, longing to hear the low rumbling of a turtle dove, but it was still quite early in the season and many had not yet arrived in the UK. I felt like an autograph hunter, waiting in the airport terminal for my favourite celebrity to arrive.

Reaching a clearing, a light breeze came on, and every rustle was overpowered by the nightingale's loud voice. I walked for hours, through sheltering woods where a photographer was capturing a green hairstreak butterfly, past never-ending hedges, around temporary pools alive with pond-skaters (turtle doves suck up the water to make crop milk for their young), all the while listening to all kinds of bird song, until I found myself back at the visitor centre. No luck. Having passed multiple bird hides – one even called the "Nightingale Hide" – the nightingale (rather ironically) seemed eager to make their presence known, and it was the turtle dove which was hiding from me. The café was a welcome sight.

Swallows, swifts and red kites performed various cinematic moves outside the IMAX window. The ranger, Alex Long, appeared and I explained my mission.

"Your best chance is probably Wrabness Nature Reserve," he said. There had already been lots of turtle dove sightings that week. I thanked him, drank up and went back to my car. Wrabness was further north than I had intended to travel, but the choice was made; I was going.

Some forty-five minutes later, I arrived. It was country lane galore. No visitor centre to take refuge in this time. I parked down a dead end in a muddy layby. In front of me was a man, trying to get a kayak down from the roof of his car, aiming to launch it on the River Stour, the banks of which lay just over a grassy mound ahead.

"Do you need any help, mate?" I asked. He politely declined, but it was as if my offer turned karma in my favour and it started. *Puuuurrrrrrrrrrr.* I all but ran up the bank, barely taking in the watery scene which opened before me and followed the low frequency. It led me across the bank and back inland, a few metres balancing across a concrete pipe, to a small pond where a little egret scanned the surface for an early supper.

Two birdwatchers were already there, a German man and a woman. I followed their line of sight up into a tall tree across the pond and there it was, bouncing on the end of a thin branch. Externally I was composed, but my heart leapt. The blushing pinks and blues were intoxicating against the greenery, like a colourful cocktail. The rumbling song was louder than I had expected, laying down a hypnotic bassline for other songbirds to harmonise with.

I sat and stared. When it flew away, I walked off down the path alongside the river, feeling a sense of elation and surprising calm wash over me – mission accomplished. After twenty minutes, "*turr-turr,*" there was that song again! Two turtle doves in one day, and it wasn't even nearly Christmas! Locating the source, this bird seemed shyer, sitting on a branch of oak overhanging dense shrubbery, musing over the skeletal skiffs whose ribs were poking out of the silty shore to my right.

I left before he did, serenaded all the way back along the river's edge to the grassy mound in front of my car. Just before I turned to leave, I looked out upon a white sailing boat with white sails, and the kayaker paddling to Suffolk.

When I go home at night just as tired as I be
I take my youngest child and I dance him on my knee.
The others come around me with their prattle-prattling toys
And that's the only comfort a working man enjoys.

My wife and I are willing and we join both in one yoke,
We live like two turtle doves and not one word provoke.
Although the times are very hard and we are very poor
Yet still we keep the raving wolf away from the door.

– 'The Honest Labourer', verses 4-5

# Two for Joy

## (*Pica pica*)

*I never met a colleen with such beauties blessed*
*Like the little Irish fairy in the magpie's nest.*

– 'The Magpie's Nest'

BLADES OF DEWY GRASS, blinding like shards of glass shattered across the rise. It is early spring, and a young man walks over the verdant common, squelching with each step. Wet socks in shoes; he knows he should have worn his walking boots. Halt! Stopped in his tracks. Something is lurking, observing, calculating, head tilting. A dark, all-seeing eye is cocked in his direction. "Good morning, Mr Magpie! How are Mrs Magpie and all the other little magpies?" These hurried words fall from his mouth, and he tips his cap as a saluting mark of respect. Displeasing a lone chatterpie is no way to start the day...

\* \* \*

As I write, over the rim of my glasses, I see gulls circling below a ceiling of dark cloud. Hordes of white-speckled starlings make trips to and from the birdfeeder, momentarily descending onto thin tree branches which bow under their weight, pinging upwards again when they cast off. But down in the garden is a single hopping bird, picking up discarded breadcrumbs. Dressed in a smart white shirt and tailcoat, it resembles an undertaker about to lead a solemn procession. It has many names but is instantly recognised by adults and children alike.

Margot Pye, Margaret's pie, Madge, maggot, Cornish pheasant, ninut, haggister and pyot. The list of regional monikers goes on, but we know her as the magpie. Together, groups of magpies are called a "mischief" and, of all the birds, this species is perhaps the most steeped in superstition.

Since time immemorial, a single magpie has been regarded as a portent of doom – historically feeding on battlegrounds, at field hospitals and regularly attending the gallows. Christian lore rumours that this species carries a drop of the devil's blood in their tongues. Apparently, if you were to cut their tongue and release the blood, the magpie would be capable of human speech. It has also been said that the magpie was the only bird not to enter Noah's Ark, instead deciding to sit on the roof and swear at the drowning world.

As well as sorrow, a solitary magpie may also bring clouds and rain according to this nineteenth-century proverb – which is akin to sorrow for many:

A single magpie in spring, foul weather will bring.

One only has to look at their appearance to understand why the magpie has been demonised in this way. Pied plumage:

black and pure white with iridescent bluey-purple wings and a gradated green lustrous tail the length of its body. They *look* dark and magical, so they must be. Right?

And so, to see a single magpie is said to bring bad luck and, according to ancient superstitions, other than saluting the only way to counter the curse is to see a crow immediately afterwards. Such ill omens are alluded to in the traditional nursery rhyme 'One for Sorrow'. First recorded in 1780 though based on superstitions dating back to at least the early sixteenth century, it describes a person's fortune after a certain number of magpies are seen. The most well-known version reads:

One for sorrow,
Two for joy,
Three for a girl,
Four for a boy,
Five for silver,
Six for gold,
Seven for a secret never to be told.

The rhyme has been chopped and changed over the years – many people have it fully memorised, like a piece of folk wisdom that gets absorbed via osmosis during our childhoods. Here's the original:

One for sorrow,
Two for mirth,
Three for a funeral
And four for birth.

In 1846, merchant and folklorist Michael Aislabie Denham extended the rhyme in his book, *Proverbs and Popular Sayings of the Seasons*:

Five for heaven
Six for hell
Seven for the devil, his own self.

Then, in the 1960s, English folkie David Dodds – mandolin player turned fly fisher – used this rhyme to create a traditional-sounding folksong called 'The Magpie', popularly recorded by The Unthanks. Apparently, one day David gave a lift to an old lady who insisted on repeating, "Devil, devil, I defy thee," and spitting on the floor of his car each time she saw a magpie. David was unimpressed considering his car was new, but it did inspire a wonderful song, with the lady's superstitious phrase forming the chorus.

\* \* \*

What is the first word that comes to mind when you hear the name 'magpie'? For many, that word is 'thief'. It is still believed by many that they are rampant tea-leaves [cockney rhyming slang for 'thieves'], just waiting until your back is turned to swoop in and steal your shiny keys and jewellery. Although scientists at Exeter University disproved their alleged kleptomaniac tendencies almost a decade ago, mud unfortunately sticks. Italian composer Gioachino Rossini even released an opera in 1817 called *The Thieving Magpie* about a household maid who is accused of stealing silver from her employers and almost hanged. She is reprieved when it is revealed that a magpie stole the loot and hid it in the church tower. More recently, the theme of a magpie stealing treasure also runs through Series 3 of *The Detectorists*, a BBC show about metal detectorists written by Mackenzie Crook (highly recommended if you haven't seen it!). In reality, however, this corvid is more likely to steal your sandwich than your silver.

Perhaps this highly intelligent bird is also condemned in folklore because they are not afraid to make themselves heard. That is never truer than when I walk my regular lap around my local woods and hear the rasping, guttural chatter from above. They seem to shout indiscriminately at the world, at each other, at their parents and at other creatures, including me. Whilst I do try to look as if I have no intention of climbing a tree to get to them, they still feel a pressing need to warn their peers of my presence. Even then, these woodland magpies seem almost shocked that I would deign to walk below them, attempting to bar the gated entrance with a wall of sound.

So, with their alleged thieving ways and a voice loud enough to betray your position to every creature for miles around, just one word comes to mind: untrustworthy. Some may say this is how the species is presented in the following song, 'The Maid and the Magpie'. I think it shows quite the opposite, but I will leave it open for you to decide. The song was originally written for music halls by W. H. Phillips in 1878 before passing into the oral tradition.

In a tiny corner of the British Library's sound archives there is a recording of this song which transports us back to a Suffolk village pub called The Blaxhall Ship in 1972[9]. Inaudible chatter and laughter from around the bar are cut through with heckles of "Go on the magpie!" and "Go on Cyril!" – calls for Cyril Poacher (1910–99), a long-faced man holding a pipe in his mouth and wearing a suit, to sing this birdy song from his repertoire.

Cyril could not have been more local, having been born at Stone Common, Blaxhall, and singing in that same pub since the late 1920s. He learnt songs as a boy on his grandfather's knee and worked on local farms until his retirement in the mid-seventies, around the time this recording was made by Keith Summers.

The noise in the pub continues even through a more authoritative shout of "ORDER PLEASE FOR THE MAGPIE!" and three knocks on the wooden table, but as soon as Cyril begins to sing, every punter falls silent. His voice is forceful, and with his country dialect he draws out the drama of each line, stressing every syllable like the song was his legacy, because he knew it was. All of the locals join in with the chorus, having heard it many times before.

### The Maid and the Magpie

Now once there was a maid kept an old magpie,
And a parson who prayed lived very close by;
When this maid met the parson they both stopped to talk
And often on the quiet they would go for cosy walks.
For her lover was a sailor, he crossed the raging main,
He promised she would be his bride when he returned again,
But still she let the parson see her home from church,
And kiss her never thinking of the magpie on the perch.

*Chorus:*
So the maid and the magpie would talk all the day.
The maid would not believe all the magpie did say,
She said, "I love the parson, but don't you tell the tar." [sailor]
And the old magpie only said, "Quar, quar!"

Now while this sailor was away or so the story goes,
This maid flirted with the parson but of course nobody knows,
Until she told the magpie when talking one day,
She'd rather have the parson now the sailor is away.
She said don't tell my secret or I'll give you the birch,

# Singing Like Larks

Every night at nine I meet the parson by the church,
The magpie only quar-quar'd as he had done before,
But he meant to tell the sailor boy when he returned on shore.

While stationed at Gibraltar the sailor so it seems,
One night whilst sleeping in his bunk he had a funny dream;
He dreamt the girl he'd left behind on dear old England's shore,
Would whilst he was away flirt with half a dozen more.
So he made his passage homeward, as quickly as could be,
He landed safely at her house but no maiden could he see;
He then talked to the magpie who was dancing on the perch,
And the magpie told him all about the parson at the church.

Now when the sailor met this maid he passed her with disdain,
She sued for breach of promise for five thousand to obtain,
They brought the magpie into court who told the truthful tale,
So to get what she required of course this maiden she did fail.
She then went to the parson but in vain for him did search,
For he knew which way the wind it blew and hooked it from
    the church;
The lawyers couldn't find him, so the case went on the shelf,
And this trickly little maiden had to dwell all by herself.

The maid and the magpie ne'er talk all the day,
For the jolly little sailor took the knowing bird away;
And now, with all his shipmates, this rare good-hearted tar,
While the magpie tells this truthful tale, he sings "Quar! Quar!"

\* \* \*

Magpies are a marmite bird: some love them, others love to
hate them. I am in the former camp, seeing through their
loud and mischievous ways to an incredible reasoning ability and endearing curiosity. It must be remembered that dark

superstitions were created by us and pinned onto unknowing birds like the magpie, and other dark birds like the crow and raven. No matter how many grave yarns are wound about them, they will continue to grace our gardens and – whilst most are told in good humour – Maggie deserves no grief for them.

In brain-to-body mass ratio, magpies are outmatched only by us humans, equalling the aquatic mammals and great apes. Tool use, game playing and grieving are just a few abilities they possess, and they are even able to recognise themselves – a trait which is uncommon in non-mammals. This was tested by placing small, coloured stickers on the breasts of some magpies and seeing whether they would pick them off when looking in a mirror. Clearly, magpies are far from bird-brained, so perhaps we should marvel at their natural abilities rather than obsess over superstitions and ill omens.

At least one traditional song agrees, called 'The Magpie's Nest'. This dreamlike song of courtship relates the beauty of the magpie. Its origin is unknown, and the song itself is only known from the singing of Annie Jane Kelly, Sarah Makem's cousin, who also lived in Keady in Co. Armagh, Northern Ireland. Like Sarah, Annie was a storehouse of old songs. Peter Kennedy recalls how she came in with her dog one evening in 1952 when he was recording Sarah, stubbed out a cigarette and delivered her unforgettable, lilting performance whilst the family watched on.

### The Magpie's Nest

For if I was a king sure I would make you my queen,
I would roll you in my arms when the meadows they are green;
Yes I'd roll you in my heart's content, I would sit you down to rest
'Longsides me Irish colleen in the magpie's nest.

# Singing Like Larks

*Chorus:*
Skiddle idle dahdle doodle idle ahdle dum
D'lidle ahdle oo dahdle idle idle dum
Skiddle idle ahdle doodle dahdle idle doodle dum
I would leave you down to rest in the magpie's nest.

For the magpie's nest it is a cottage neat and clean,
It stands 'longsides the Shannon where the meadows they are
   green.
But I never met a colleen with such beauties blessed
Like the little Irish fairy in the magpie's nest.

For I have wandered all through Kerry, I have wandered all
   through Clare,
From Dublin down to Galway from there to God knows where.
But I never met a colleen with such beauties blessed
Like the little Irish fairy in the magpie's nest.

The quiet and measured field recording of Annie can be heard on an album called *As I Roved Out (Field Trip-Ireland)*. Each lyric stands firm, tested under its own weight, lingering like a morning mist. It feels like you are there with Annie, inside that little Keady cottage, having popped across the high street to hear an evening song.

In reality, the magpie's nest is perhaps the most sophisticated of all the birds. It is lined with mud and vegetation, domed beautifully with branches and twigs, then built up and over the top to form a roof – like the neat cottage described in the song. Nestled well above the ground in thorny bushes or tall trees, this is where females lay about six greenish-blue eggs, matching their sheening plumage. Such a unique nest prompted not only this folk song, but an English fairy tale also called 'The

Magpie's Nest', edited and published by Joseph Jacobs in 1854. Jacobs was a folklorist inspired by the Brothers Grimm and was a leading authority on the subject in his day. Adapted from Jacobs' *English Fairy Tales*[10], the tale goes:

*Once upon a time when pigs spoke rhyme, and monkeys chewed tobacco, and hens took snuff to make them tough, and ducks went quack, quack, quack, O!*

*All the birds of the air came to Madge Magpie and asked her to teach them how to build a nest, for she was the cleverest of them all. They gathered round to watch how it was done. First, she took some mud and made a round cake with it.*

*"Oh, I see," said the thrush, and away it flew. That is how thrushes build their nests today.*

*The magpie then took some twigs and arranged them round in the mud.*

*"Now I know all about it," said the blackbird, and off he flew. That is how the blackbirds build nests.*

*Then the magpie put another layer of mud over the twigs.*

*"Oh, that's quite obvious," said the wise owl, and off he went. Owls have never made better nests since.*

*After this the magpie took more twigs and twined them round the outside.*

*"The very thing!" said the sparrow, and away he went. Sparrows make rather slovenly nests to this day.*

*After this, Madge took some feathers and lined the cosy nest with them.*

*"That suits me," cried the starling, and off it flew. They have made comfortable nests since then.*

*So this demonstration went on, and on, with each bird taking away a piece of nest-building knowledge, but none of them waiting patiently until the end. Madge Magpie went on working, without looking up, until the only bird remaining was the turtle dove, who had not paid any attention. Each time the magpie took a twig, the maddening dove advised, "Turrr, turrr, take twooo." After placing the final twig, Madge eventually snapped, "One is enough, I tell you!" She got angry and flew away, refusing to teach the birds how to build a nest ever again. That is why different birds build their nests differently.*

\* \* \*

To this very day, an English tradition holds that a single magpie should be greeted with a salutation. It is customary to politely bid the bird a good morning and ask after his wife and nestlings. Mr Magpie, General or Captain are some suitable addresses, for his name demands to be spoken with respect. Some even flap their wings upon seeing a magpie to imitate a second, attempting to avoid the mournful tidings reported in 'One for Sorrow'.

When I am leading Forest School sessions, the children are never short of surprises. A class of Year 2s and I were out one cold afternoon in a woodland site, sitting around a log circle getting ready to roast marshmallows. I started with a Nature Spots mindfulness activity. This is where each child goes off and finds their own space in the woods to sit or stand quietly and simply take in the wildlife around them. Looking. Listening. Breathing gently in and out. After five minutes I called everyone back to the log circle:

"ONE, TWO, THREE, BACK TO ME!"

"ONE, TWO, BACK TO YOU!" they shouted in reply.

We passed around the talking stick – a whittled piece of horse chestnut which gives the wielder the right to speak to the group – sharing the things we had seen and heard in our Nature Spot. One boy said, "I heard the wind through the trees," another said, "I saw a ladybird," another shyly whispered, "Magpie." On hearing this, the seven-year-old girl on the log next to me immediately reeled off the entirety of 'One for Sorrow' to the group but could not recall where she had learnt it.

Clearly, most children have no trouble identifying this species. In the height of summer, I walked across the school playground towards the large field with around ten children from the After-School Club in tow. Our brisk passing momentarily parted birds and squirrels who had ventured onto the hop-scotch-tattooed concrete to pick at the daily harvest of sandwich crumbs rained down at lunchtime. A crow flew off with an apple core. The kids and I played some evening football in the lee of ancient oaks until a magpie hopped out onto the grass. Out of curiosity I asked them, "What bird do you think that is?"

"A magpie!" they all answered together.

The ball rolled to a stop. We watched, transfixed, for a minute until the bird stretched out its white-tipped wings and disappeared into the canopy. "Who's in goal?" a boy asked, ending the moment by recommencing the game. Sunlight flared through my sunglasses and the mild air was bursting with laughter, orchestral birdsong and chatter. There may have only been one magpie, but on such days, there is enough joy to go around.

# Heffle Cuckoo Fair

## (*Cuculus canorus*)

*The cuckoo she's a pretty bird, she sings as she flies,*
*She brings us glad tidings, and tells us no lies*

'Bunclody'

THE ATTIC WARBLER pours her throat,
Responsive to the cuckoo's note,
The untaught harmony of spring:
While whisp'ring pleasure as they fly,
Cool zephyrs thro' the clear blue sky
Their gather'd fragrance fling.

– 'Ode on the Spring' (1742), Thomas Gray

One cloudless morning in April, you leave the coat on its hanger and venture outside to find that the world has awakened. The air seems lighter, the sun higher and, stretching your eyes into the regreened distance, the colours appear more buzzingly vibrant. Leaves folded into last autumn's woodland floor return triumphantly to their branches, rising like hibernators out of winter's heavy slumber. "*Cuck-ooo*" plays on repeat. Oh, yes, there are some mild days to be had in March, but this strikes each sense differently. The season has changed overnight.

The cuckoo's call has forever marked the hopeful tipping of winter into spring and signalled the early strains of the fast-approaching summer. *Cunculus canorus* stars in the oldest known English song, 'Sumer is icumen in', dating from the mid-thirteenth century and included in one of the world's most famous medieval manuscripts, *Harley* 978, looked after by the British Library. The cuckoo is front and centre at the very birth of our ancient song tradition and, whilst unimaginable change has occurred since this song was scribed, our symbol of spring remains.

The lyrics of the song are written in the Wessex dialect of Middle English and the music is presented in square nota-tion on a six-line red stave. Once belonging to the monks of Reading Abbey, *Harley* 978 also contains medical texts, a glos-sary of herbs, poems and fables. The first letters of the words 'Sumer' and 'Sing' are inked onto the pale parchment in alter-nating royal blue and red.

Sumer is icumen in
Lhude sing cuccu
Groweþ sed
and bloweþ med
and springþ þe wde nu
Sing cuccu

This is the first known use of the word "cuckoo" in written English. The full translated version reads:

# Singing Like Larks

Summer has arrived,
Loudly sing, cuckoo!
The seed is growing
And the meadow is blooming,
And the wood is coming into leaf now,
Sing, cuckoo!

The ewe is bleating after her lamb,
The cow is lowing after her calf;
The bullock is prancing,
The stag cavorting,
Sing merrily, cuckoo!

Cuckoo, cuckoo,
You sing well, cuckoo,
Never stop now.
Sing, cuckoo, now; sing, cuckoo;
Sing, cuckoo; sing, cuckoo, now!

Much dispute surrounds the "stag cavorting" line, written in Middle English as "bucke uerteþ". In modern times the phrase has been interpreted by some to mean "the billy-goat farting", revealing a comedic vulgarity, or simply an indifference to familiar farmyard occurrences in medieval culture. If this translation is accurate, then 'Sumer is icumen in' contains the oldest record of this mild profanity used in written English! Prudish Victorian anthologists made desperate changes to the line, attempting to make it tolerable for the sensibilities of their day. It was omitted from many schoolbooks, supposedly shielding youngsters from so-called indecency.

Although this song sounds like an outright celebration of the summer, it is actually a springtime anthem for a migratory bird returning to our shores. The simple explanation is that the Middle English "sumer" was used to represent a far broader part of the year than our "summer", reaching backwards into the spring. The lyrics have been related to a French genre of poetry called the *reverdie*, literally meaning "regreening", where the speaker encounters the personified spring, often depicted as a woman, and compliments her wonderous beauty by calling upon springtime figureheads like the cuckoo.

'Sumer is icumen in' is a Medieval English round (a type of "canon"), meaning that as one singer begins, another starts just afterwards, and so on, until a whole host of staggered voices are harmonising together on different lines. Several spectral voices merge on the lyrical ridges of powerful notes and diverge on others, much like a murmuration, with lines of shared song shaking the woodwormed eaves of thatched cottages and vibrating the stained glass windows of cold limestone churches; less gravestones are planted at this time of year, more flowers.

Such secular songs offer a vague and usually romanticised window into the life of the ordinary medieval man and woman – but a window, nonetheless, that we can peer through and find them unchanged. Whilst life was harsher then, ruled by the weather and high rates of mortality, these lyrics suggest that the backbreaking labours of spring months (chiefly ploughing, sowing, weeding and – indeed – bird scaring) were offset by the joyful return of the light. Their imagined ancient voices carry almost a millennium's worth of undiluted enthusiasm for the glorious return of the evening sun over furrowed fields. Darkness has ended. Now is the time for blooming meadows, fair sweethearts and calling cuckoos.

# Singing Like Larks

\* \* \*

The cuckoo comes in April,
She sings the month of May.
She changes tune in the middle of June,
And in July she flies away.[11]

After spending the winter months in Central Africa, cuckoos return to the UK in mid-April. In the Middle Ages, it was widely believed that cuckoos literally brought the season with them from their travels – but that is not all. Migration was not well understood, so many thought this species transformed into sparrowhawks during the winter, which is understandable considering their likeness – both sleek-bodied and long-tailed with a similar size and colouring.

You need only to speak this species' common name to be reminded of the male's iconic two-tone song. Females make a harsh bubbling sound like an avian chuckle, and a minority are rusty red, set apart from their ashen peers. Grey, barred underparts resemble icing which has not yet been feathered. That classic cuckoo image comes to mind, with a single bird perching in a treetop with its long tail stretched backwards and pointed wings held low in song posture, looking like a gymnast steadying themselves after a dismount.

Their April arrival is eagerly awaited, with countryfolk pacing woodland margins with their ears cocked, listening out for the "wandering voice"[12] (as Wordsworth described it) of spring's first cuckoo echoing through the trees. Hearing one is like a seasonal switch in the mind, a reminder to plan ahead for the growing season. In Yorkshire a common response to their call was: "When you hear the cuckoo shout, it's time to plant your taties out." In rural Shropshire, as soon as the first cuckoo of spring was heard, the farm workers would down tools and drink beer for the remainder of the day. Even now, a letter to *The Times* from a reader marks the first sighting each year.

Trying to locate a cuckoo from its voice alone is like chasing the end of a rainbow – once you think you have found it, it moves. I have heard them but, sadly, have only actually seen this Redlist species protruding from the cuckoo clocks lining the walls of the German Market that my local garden centre runs each December. The British Trust for Ornithology have been tracking cuckoos since 2011 and have witnessed a sharp decline with over seventy percent of cuckoos lost in Britain over the last twenty-five years.[13]

Despite this devastating decline, the cuckoo has stirred up more folklore than most other birds. In the village of Marsden, West Yorkshire, the locals still celebrate the cuckoo's return with "Cuckoo Day Festival" – a craft fair and village procession which includes a maypole for Morris dancers to perform their vibrant displays. In the smaller village of Wing, Rutland, it is said that the villagers once caged a cuckoo in an attempt to prolong the warmer weather and keep winter at bay. However, when the cuckoo escaped and winter returned, the villagers became known in Rutland as Wing Fools for attempting it.

Plenty of superstition surrounds this species too; simply seeing a cuckoo before breakfast was once said to be an omen of bad luck. Such old wives' tales have largely fallen away, never to be missed, but in the little market town of Heathfield, in East Sussex, there is a tradition which surely would be: Heffle Cuckoo Fair.

# Singing Like Larks

In 1315, the Bishop of Chichester obtained permission to hold a weekly market and annual fair in Heffle, an ancient name for Heathfield. A fair has been held on April 14th, sometimes called "First Cuckoo Day", for centuries to welcome in the spring – although now it takes place on a Saturday. Groups of people parade through Cade Street, some holding garlands of flowers, others dressed in colourful costumes, but all waving to the lining crowds. Fiddles, accordions, drums and jingling bells play in time with Morris dancers who *clank* their sticks together as their hankies and yellow ribbons come alive with movement.

Travelling people once gathered in the town for the fair and, each year, one of the oldest women amongst them would be chosen as Dame Heffle – today she is chosen from the villagers. Wearing a witch-like black hat with a long feather, Dame Heffle holds a toaster-sized wicker basket which everyone gathers around. It is loosely weaved in the middle so that the dark plumage of the two cuckoos within can just about be seen. At the height of anticipation, the basket is thrown open, and the birds fly up and out. Spring has officially arrived.

As eyes return to earth, the merry crowd melts into the various delights of the fair, which continues into the small hours.

Heffle Cuckoo Fair
Tell it to the locked-up trees,
Cuckoo, bring your song here!
Warrant, Act and Summons, please,
For Spring to pass along here!
Tell old Winter, if he doubt,
Tell him squat and square—a!
Old Woman!

Old Woman!
Old Woman's let the Cuckoo out
At Heffle Cuckoo Fair—a!

March has searched and April tried—
'Tisn't long to May now,
Not so far to Whitsuntide,
And Cuckoo's come to stay now!
Hear the valiant fellow shout
Down the orchard bare—a!
Old Woman!
Old Woman!
Old Woman's let the Cuckoo out
At Heffle Cuckoo Fair—a!

When your heart is young and gay
And the season rules it—
Work your works and play your play
'Fore the Autumn cools it!
Kiss you turn and turn about,
But my lad, beware—a!
Old Woman!
Old Woman!
Old Woman's let the Cuckoo out
At Heffle Cuckoo Fair—a!

The famous poet Rudyard Kipling was inspired by this Heathfield ceremony, having lived in Sussex for many years. He wrote 'Cuckoo Song' in 1909, which was later set to music by folk singer Peter Bellamy in the 1980s and named 'Heffle Cuckoo Fair'. Just like that, this song was born. Even though it is not technically traditional, it still feels it to me. Without Bellamy's rendition, this bizarre ornithological ritual would have passed me by. At least in my mind, this piece lies somewhere between the old and the new – blurring the lines between poem, song and tradition.

Heffle Cuckoo Fair continues annually, strong as ever, and all proceeds go to charity. In recent years, the fair has had craft stalls, Romani wagons, vintage cars, a dog show and more! Sadly, cuckoos are now so few and far between in Britain that collared doves or racing pigeons are used in their place. Onlookers must use their imaginations.

\* \* \*

Peter Bellamy set many of Kipling's poems to music, most of which required little musical arrangement as they were originally written in the style of old English ballads. Born in North Norfolk in 1944, Peter was always a creative individual and had a dry wit on stage. In his younger days he painted a flamboyant artistic image, wearing his long hair in a ribboned ponytail and donning lacy-collared shirts, floral trousers and cowboy-esque hats. And yet, despite his contemporary appearance, the nasal vibrato of his warbling voice has taken its unique place in British folk music history.

In the only video recording that I have ever found of Peter – a camera copy of a grainy VHS tape from the 1980s – he is being interviewed at home wearing double denim and a blue waistcoat to match, contrasting with the dandelion-yellow walls behind him. Row upon row of music tapes line the shelves which span the room above his head, as he eagerly sits forward on his sofa next to a key-worn concertina, anticipating each question. He explains that, in his early teens during the 1950s, he started out by listening to skiffle music, an American genre drawing on folk, country, blues, bluegrass and jazz music.

Skiffle caught his imagination and, whilst his friends natu-rally followed from that into rock and roll, he dug for its roots. American folk music is what he found, through musicians like Pete Seeger and Woody Guthrie, before realising at seventeen that "England has folk music too". Peter's route into folk music is not dissimilar to my own – first listening to American per-formers like Johnny Cash and Bob Dylan, then Irish folk music inspired by my Irish granny, before discovering that there are great treasure troves of songs closer to home.

Although he never criticised, Peter tried not to modernise traditional songs with new instrumentation and rhythms like contemporary folk rock bands such as Steeleye Span, Fairport Convention and Oysterband, choosing instead to focus on vocal quality. As he would say, it's all about the "song and the singer" and not about the arrangement. You may have heard a song thousands of times before but, when he delivers it, you can never guess where the melody will take you. With just his voice and a microphone, Peter made old songs new again.

Dropping out of art school in his early twenties, Peter became a professional singer in 1965 when he formed a trio called The Young Tradition, consisting of himself, Royston Wood and Heather Wood (no relation). Their powerful close harmonies represented a fresh new generation projecting ancient lyrics into a modern age.

The Young Tradition showed great respect for the British folk singing tradition, even studying harmony with the Copper Family, but they also retained a healthy desire to produce something unique. For a folk scene which had doubled down on soloists and instrumentation, they boldly reintroduced unaccompanied harmony singing, and with great success. The group lasted only four years, releasing three albums in a whirlwind of youthful creativity. They split because Peter wished to concentrate on traditional English music, whilst the others were focused on medieval music. He became a soloist, eventually in more ways than one.

Tragically, Peter died by suicide in 1991, after a period of depression and isolation. He was penniless, with no upcoming gigs or folk club bookings and – as a performer, not a businessman – he felt embarrassed to ask for them. Upon enquiring after how he was, fellow folk singing friends recall him holding up his diary and silently leafing through the blank, empty pages. His widow, Jenny, spoke of how he spent a whole day before his death listening intently to every record he'd ever released, saying at the end, "But I am good. What the hell has gone wrong?" Peter was part of a golden age of folk music, but when it waned he was starved of the oxygen that all great artists crave: the appreciation of his art.

For those new to the world of folk music, Bellamy is a great place to start. He was influenced by such a vast array of genres and singers, so his colossal musical output is like the centre of a glistening web from which you can pick any musical strand and work outwards, questing to find the original singer, and from there a whole honeypot of previously untapped music. I have spent countless hours embarking on these journeys of discovery and I would not change it for the world.

\* \* \*

When farmers walk and work their fields, birds are often their only companions. They act as life partners and sole witnesses to tiresome days in what can otherwise be an extremely lonely occupation. A debt is repaid, and companionship acknowledged, within traditional agricultural songs like 'The Brisk Young Ploughboy' – a harvest supper song from the Coppers' repertoire, expressing fondness and gratitude for this enduring friendship. For rural communities, the cuckoo's oddly human voice proclaiming that winter is finally over is a welcome sound indeed.

> Now seedtime being over the fields look fresh and gay
> There's merry lads to mow the grass while damsels make the hay.
> The small birds sing on every tree, the cuckoo joins sweet harmony,
> All welcome here as you may see, the brave ploughboy.[14]

\* \* \*

Where does the cuckoo sleep? Most of them make no nest at all. In fact, they are the only British bird not to rear their own young. As a brood parasite, the female sneakily lays her eggs in the nests of other birds when they are away from home: one egg in each host nest, and up to fifty nests per breeding season! They will usually choose the nest of the bird species that raised them – most often the dunnock, meadow pipit, pied wagtail or reed warbler. Females tend to target one species and stick to it for life, disguising their eggs (although larger) to look similar to the host's – in the case of the dunnock, a beautiful bluish green.

Does the deception stop there? No chance. Adults mimic the cry of a predatory sparrowhawk, spooking other birds away from their chosen nests and giving the female cuckoo time to deposit her treasure without being attacked. When the egg hatches after around eleven days, the cuckoo hatchling may then seize the opportunity to push out any host eggs or chicks from the nest. Sometimes they are raised alongside the host chicks, and, like big babies, the young cuckoo looks humorously out of proportion compared to the likes of a meadow pipit, growing to two or three times the size of their adopted parents – imagine the shopping bill!

It was once thought that cuckoos were unable to raise their own young due to defective anatomy, and so other birds kindly stepped up to help them. Darwin overturned this quaint view, suggesting that the target species were in fact tricked into raising them. Today, the cuckoo is in a sort of evolutionary arms race as its victims get better and better at spotting alien eggs in their nest, forcing the cuckoo to become more and more accurate in its mimicry.

Despite the non-existence of such a structure, 'The Cuckoo's Nest' is the name of both a bawdy song and a Morris dance tune, with the former using the image as a thinly disguised sex symbol. Just one verse reveals all:

As I was a-walking one morning in May
I met a pretty fair maid and unto her did say:
"I'll tell you me mind, it's for love I am inclined
And me inclination lies in your cuckoo's nest."[15]

The term "cuckold" is closely related to the bird's natural behaviour, referring to the husband of an adulterous wife. It was often used by Shakespeare: "I will chop her into messes! Cuckold me?" shouts Othello, when led to believe that his love, Desdemona, has been unfaithful to him. However, he did not invent the word – it originated way back around 1250. The general idea is that, like the cuckoo's unfortunate targets, a cuckold may unwittingly invest parental effort into offspring which are not genetically their own.

Broadsides commonly played on the cuckoo's deceit, using its call as a warning to husbands with disloyal wives. 'The Cuckowes Comendation', c. 1625, is one such rhyme, although I believe the tune is lost:

> The smith on his anvil the iron hard doth ding:
> He cannot heare the cuckoo though he loud doth sing
> In pointing of plow harnesse, he labours till he sweat,
> While another in his forge at home may steale a private heat.

Such notions of infidelity crop up again in one of the most poignant songs ever written – 'The Maid of Bunclody'. This song has been in my own repertoire for years, but I never fully realised the cuckoo's significance within it until writing this chapter.

The Maid of Bunclody[16]

> Oh were I at the moss house where the birds do increase,
> At the foot of Mount Leinster or some silent place,
> By the streams of Bunclody where all pleasures do meet,
> And all I would ask is one kiss from you sweet.
>
> Oh the streams of Bunclody they flow down so free,
> By the streams of Bunclody I am longing to be,
> A-drinking strong liquor in the height of my cheer,
> Here's a health to Bunclody and the lass I love dear.
>
> The cuckoo she's a pretty bird, she sings as she flies,
> She brings us glad tidings, and tells us no lies,
> She sucks the young birds' eggs for to make her voice clear
> And the more she cries "Cuckoo" the summer draws near.

# Singing Like Larks

Tis why my love left me as you may understand,
For tis she has a freehold and I have no land,
She has great store of riches and a large sum of gold
And everything fitting a house to uphold.

So farewell my dear father and mother adieu
My sister and brother, farewell unto you,
I am bound for America my fortune to try,
When I think on Bunclody, now I am ready to die.

Allegedly, these lyrics were penned centuries ago by an emigrant of Bunclody, but I first heard it sung by Luke Kelly – the ideal voice for a song running deep with incurable sorrow. Bunclody is a small town in Co. Wexford, cleaved by streams that babble through the town. The song is simple – the lyricist misses his home. It's a ballad that Luke wished to be remembered for, taught to him by a teacher living in the town.

For all the cuckoo's anticipated arrival, this summer visitor is just that – a visitor – and by late June most have flown south, returning to Africa. Whoever wrote 'The Maid of Bunclody' was keenly aware of their fleeting appearance on these shores and called on the natural world and the simple power of words to extoll the beauty of love and our own defencelessness against the falling sands within time's fragile hourglass; the songwriter was not found wanting.

### The Bonny Cuckoo
My bonny cuckoo, I tell thee true
That through the groves I'll rove with you;
I'll rove with you until the next spring
And then my cuckoo shall sweetly sing.

## Heffle Cuckoo Fair

The ash and the hazel shall mourning say,
O bonny cuckoo, don't go away;
Don't go away, but tarry here,
And sing for us throughout the year.
Cuckoo, cuckoo, pray tarry here,
And make the spring last all the year.

*

*I'll go down in some lonesome valley*
*Where no man on earth shall e'er me find,*
*Where the pretty little small birds do change their voices,*
*And every moment blows blusterous wind.*

— Banks of the Sweet Primroses, *verse 5*

# Chickens in the Garden

## (*Gallus gallus domesticus*)

*"If this be true," King Herod said,*
*"That you be telling me,*
*That roasted fowl that's in the dish*
*Shall crow full fences three."*

'Herod and the Cock'

THERE ARE NO CHICKENS AT SEA. Except, perhaps, for those belonging to Mother Carey. She is the personification of storms, calling ships to wreck and pulling unfortunate sailors to their watery graves deep in Davy Jones' locker. Mother Carey is a broom-riding witch-like figure who has been feared by sailors since at least the eighteenth century and is connected to one bird – the chicken. But not all is as it seems…

Preceding even the far-flung voyaging days of Captain Cook 200 years ago, these mystical nautical chickens associated with

# Chickens in the Garden

Mother Carey have long been the talk of able seamen, navigators, officers and captains alike. When Darwin sailed on the *HMS Beagle* in the 1830s, he made a note in his journal one fine day in late March about the joys of sailing: "There is little to interrupt one, for instance since leaving Bahia the only living things that we have seen were a few sharks and Mother Carys [Carey's] chickens."

As you may have guessed, Mother Carey's Chickens are not chickens at all, but rather a nautical name for storm petrels. These pelagic birds infamously presage storms – as their name suggests – leading to their reputation as heralds of Mother Carey and the shipwrecks that ensue from her wrath. Fortunately, this was not the fate of the *HMS Beagle*. It was once common sealore amongst sailors that the severity of a storm could be determined by the number of "stormies" (as these birds were sometimes known) seen beforehand, whilst others thought that petrels lived within hurricanes, directing the storms themselves. Some even perceived these brown-black birds as the friendly souls of dead seamen, warning of coming danger.

Storm petrels are entirely oceanic outside of the breeding season, feeding their chicks at sea with an oily orange regurgitated liquid – the remains of small fish, squid and zooplankton. As chickens are a staple on the land, I can see how the sea-staying storm petrel became their maritime equivalent. Kipling wrote a poem about Mother Carey's Chickens called 'Anchor Song' in 1893 which, like 'Heffle Cuckoo Fair', Peter Bellamy later recorded as a folk song. The chorus goes:

Well, ah fare you well; we can stay no more with you, my love –
Down, set down your liquor and your girl from off your knee;
For the wind has come to say:

# Singing Like Larks

"You must take me while you may,
If you'd go to Mother Carey,
(Walk her down to Mother Carey!)
Oh, we're bound to Mother Carey where she feeds her chicks at
   sea!"[17]

*     *     *

It is worth reminding myself that this is not a book about song-birds, but rather a book about birds in song. The chicken (refer-ring to an actual land chicken, rather than a storm petrel!) is not known for its musicality, apart from the lute-strumming rooster narrator playing Alan-a-Dale in Disney's 1973 ani-mated feature film *Robin Hood*. Alan-a-Dale is a figure in Robin Hood legend; a wandering minstrel, who became part of Robin's band of Merry Men.

In a scene during the Disney film, the rooster, perched in an illuminated letter on the page of an old storybook, sums up the role of a folk singer remarkably well. He tells us that he's a minstrel, and explains that it's his job to tell stories, whether from the present or past, usually in song. He describes himself as a kind of early version of a folk singer.

Alan-a-Dale then goes on to sing a song about Robin Hood walking through the forest with Little John, the pair of them laughing and chatting, reminiscing about all sorts of things and having fun. The verse ends with "Oo-de-lally, oo-de-lally, golly what a day!" It's all very relaxed and playful until the sheriff and his men turn up in pursuit, firing their bows and arrows at the pair. The song can be found on Youtube (and of course is best seen in the film itself).

# Chickens in the Garden

With this exception in mind, chickens are far from tuneful. They mainly symbolise sacrifice, which is understandable considering how many are enjoyed each Sunday across the dinner table. Having existed in their domesticated form for around 8000 years, these descendants of the tropical-coloured red junglefowl (which still run wild in Southeast Asia) are incredibly useful to humans. A chicken can provide meat, eggs, insect and weed control, and even companionship. Such a diverse range of uses has made this feathered fowl the most common bird in the world, outnumbering humans by an estimated three-to-one.

Ultimately, chickens are a farm animal, and that is exactly where they are placed in folk songs – on the farm. But just because their face fits, I hesitate to assume that this is the only reason they appear in agricultural songs. After all, "mother hens" are masters of nurturance and affection, and this song of courtship is filled with such loving virtues:

Chickens in the Garden
When first I came down Yorkshire not many years ago,
I met with a little Yorkshire lass and I'd have you all to know,
That she was so blithe, so buxom, so beautiful and gay,
Now listen while I tell you what her Daddy used to say,

*Chorus (repeated after each verse):*
"Oh treat my daughter decent, don't do her any harm.
And when I die I'll leave you both my tiny little farm.
My cow, my pigs, my sheep, my goats, my stock, my field and barn,
And all the little chickens in the garden."

Well, when first I came to court the girl she was so awful shy.
She never said a blooming word when other folks stood by,

But as soon as we were on our own, well, she bade me name the
  day,
Now listen while I tell you what her Daddy used to say,

Well at last I wed this Yorkshire lass, so pleasing to me mind,
And I did prove true to her so she's proved true in kind.
We have three bairns, they're grown up now, there's a grand-
  bairn on the way,
And when I look into their eyes I can hear their grandaddy say,

Originally called 'The Farmer's Daughter', the simplicity of
this song is pleasing. As far as I can tell, there are no double
meanings or hidden subtexts, just a pleasant story that washes
over you. Versions have been collected in and around Essex,
and up in Cumbria – northern and southern England. You can
likely guess which version of the song is included above. It was
written by American songwriter James Allan Bland in 1879,
just two years before he spent twenty years in London, likely
bringing this tune over with him.

Not every farming song is so strait-laced. 'I Went to Market'
is scarce in print but was sung in pubs all over Britain, mainly
due to the simple comedy of the word "cock" being repeated
over and over.

And me cock went cock a cock a cock a doodle doo
And after every farmer's cock did my cock crow.

* * *

'ull, a port city where river meets estuary. The short, rounded
syllable is shot like a cannonball from the back of the throat,
with no need for the "H" at the front. This was the home of The

Watersons, with whom I associate 'Chickens in the Garden' entirely. Yorkshire born and bred, they are one of the most famous families in English folk music, singing with thick accents harmoniously woven together as tight as the knit of a fisherman's gansey jumper. Middle sibling, Mike Waterson (1941-2011), sings this song, and his low, flattened vowels set it firmly in Northern England.

'The Watersons' as a singing group began with three young orphans: Norma – eldest and de facto leader – Mike and Elaine (known as "Lal") Waterson. Their mother died in the late 1940s, and their father ten days later. All that remained were the three of them sitting around their grandmother's fire. Self-reliant Norma had to become mother to her two younger siblings at eight years old, and folk music adopted them all.

"Grandmother was the beginning," said Norma, sitting in her cosy sitting room during a 2007 interview. Part Irish Traveller, Grandmother was the dynastic taproot, moving the family songs (amongst others) onto these youngsters. It was just what they needed. A feeling that they were part of something bigger and older than themselves, gluing them together with musical dependency.

First, they sang hunting songs around Grandmother's blazing fire, and then hymns and carols, all to stave off bedtime for another hour. Later, in the 1960s, they took to the coffee bars and pubs of Hull, initially as a skiffle group. The three of them, along with their cousin John Harrison – from a family of fishermen – were known for a time as "The Folksons" before realising that all they needed was their last name and the music. Even on stage, they never felt like a band or group, but a family, a unit. The Watersons. They understood the world and their place within it. Backed by centuries of musical tradition, they had the confidence to be unashamedly themselves, giving off an air of "if you don't like us, don't listen".

One can only imagine how difficult it would have been to penetrate this family thicket, but that is exactly what Martin Carthy did in 1972 when he married Norma. He was an old friend, accompanying her on guitar in the sixties. As if entering such a close family group wasn't hard enough, his transition into the fold was made even harder by the fact that he was, as Martin put it himself, "just a southern bloke". But his own musical ability, popularity and love of folk songs is unquestionable – twice winning BBC 2's Folk Singer of the Year Award – and, with patience on both sides, he found his place amongst the group. Martin attests in a home interview they all did together:

> *"Well, the thing I had to understand straight off is that any fourth member of The Watersons is going to be an outsider. The three were thick as thieves and there's no way you're going to get inside. So the only thing you can do is hover round the outside and fit in where you can. And eventually the door opens a crack…"*

In 1966, about two years after their formation, the BBC commissioned a black-and-white documentary about the young group, aware that they were spearheading a folk revival. Called *Travelling for a Living – A Musical Profile of the Watersons*, it follows them as they tour the UK folk club circuit in their old smoke-filled van. Norma drives, looking out from underneath her jet-black beatnik bob. Mike lights a cigarette in the back and says, "Are we swapping round luv?"

"No we're not," replies Norma.

"Yes we are! You've had about fifty miles."

The documentary's narrator, Derrick Knight, explains how the traditional music they were singing no longer exists in living form, but only in odd corners of memory. Just one generation before the family were all either traveller, tinker or farmer, but many of the trades and ways of life described in old songs had largely disappeared.

The ploughman walking lopsided behind his oxen (one foot down in the furrow), waggoners, coopers, smithies and many more traditional trades and heritage crafts now exist only in the collected recordings, notes and jottings which are treasured in Cecil Sharp House (the home of the English Folk Dance and Song Society). And yet, from these "warm ashes" The Watersons managed to create music which felt genuine and very much alive.

They never learnt to read music, but simply felt it. If one member could not reach the main note, they sang a harmony. A springtime celebratory song called 'Hal-an-Tow' is included in the documentary, which has been clipped and wound up on YouTube. Scrolling down, a comment underneath the video makes me smile. A man claims that his folk choir leader used to describe the tone she wanted for various songs by referencing Norma's magnificently open and unrestrained voice. If it was a quiet song, then she might say, "We only need thirty-five percent Norma for this one," and the percentage increased as the songs got louder and more triumphant.

Mike Waterson – "a dreamer" – admits, in a 1983 BBC documentary *The Good Old Way*, that "Our only claim to being traditional is the tradition of singing together. Not the songs, the songs we learnt. The songs are from books and traditional singers but the process we learnt as a family." A criticism of this is that you get the tradition second-hand. That's good enough for me. A second, third or fourth-hand tradition is better than none at all.

\* \* \*

Freedom, to me, is popping in my earphones and pressing shuffle. I sometimes find it easier to edit my own writing whilst listening to unfamiliar music. For one, it stops me from singing along, but it is also a fabulous route to musical discovery. After a while, the world falls away and a trance-like state of editing takes hold – just me, the words on the page and the music. Fast-paced songs like Kate Rusby's 'Sir Eglamore' spur me on, conjuring the same feeling as driving along on a warm day with the windows down. Momentum builds. No wonder they call her the Barnsley Nightingale. Hours happily pass and, forgetting the clock, my fingers dance across the laptop keyboard, only occasionally glancing out of the back doors to watch the birds on feeders.

It was during one of these editing adventures that bright instrumentation was suddenly replaced by the simplicity of four voices, stopping me in my tracks. Dragged from concentration, I clicked on my phone screen to find out what it was, reading: 'Herod and the Cock' from *Frost & Fire: A Calendar of Ritual and Magical Songs*. It was The Watersons' first album from 1965. It sounds primally old, utterly enchanted and showcases their bone-jolting elemental power on a balladry journey through folklore and ancient seasonal celebrations. What an introduction to their music. I have had them on repeat since.

Herod and the Cock
There was a star in David's land,
In David's land appeared;
And in king Herod's bedroom
So bright it did shine there.

The Wise Men they soon spied it,
They told the king on high,
That a princely babe was born that night,
No man could ever destroy.

If this be true, king Herod said,
That you being telling me,
This roasted fowl that's in the dish
Shall crow full fences three.

Well the fowl soon feathered and thrustened well,
By the work of God's own hands,
Three times that roasted cock did crow
In the dish where he did stand.

A.L. Lloyd explains that this short ballad carol is based on a legend of St Stephen who proves the birth of Christ by causing the roast chicken in Herod's dish to rise and crow "*Christus natus est*", meaning "Christ is born" – for this Stephen was supposedly stoned for his pains and martyred. Arcanely, "fences" is used to mean the fields the fences contain, so the final line of the third verse means that the cock's crow could be heard three fields away.

Whilst their devotion to the genre never waned as individuals, The Watersons as a singing unit were always on and off. In 1968, they split for four years when Norma went to work as a disc jockey on a radio station on Montserrat. When Lal

Waterson sadly passed away very suddenly in 1998, the whole family was shaken, and Norma performed more frequently with her husband as part of Waterson–Carthy, rather than using the name The Watersons. The original name was only revived for special occasions and events, like their 2007 appearance at the Royal Albert Hall. Waterson–Carthy included Norma and Martin's daughter, Eliza Carthy. Named after Norma's grandmother, Eliza continues on the incredible tradition that her parents cared for so well.

Until very recently, Norma and Martin lived together in Robin Hood's Bay, close to Whitby in Yorkshire, where the town trickles down the hillside towards the cobbled slipway and ammonitic shore of murky Liassic shales. Mike Waterson died in 2011, and Norma died only a few days before the writing of this sentence, aged eighty-two in early 2022.

A rugged toughness rings through Norma's voice, rising from the heart and circling around the harmonies, whipping up like the northern winds. She was the brusque but tender matriarch of a musical dynasty who gave her life to the music she adored, swaying freely as she sang. What a legacy she leaves behind.

\* \* \*

Staying in Yorkshire, the next traditional song – also sung by The Watersons – is about an unfortunate blood sport. It is called 'The Holbeck Moor Cockfight', otherwise known simply as 'The Cockfight' or 'The Bonny Grey'. Broadsides containing the lyrics were published in the mid-nineteenth century:

### The Holbeck Moor Cockfight

Come all of you cockers far and near,
I'll tell you of a cock-fight, the when and where,
On Holbeck Moor, as I've heard say,
Between a black and a bonny grey.

Twelve men from Hounslow Town they came,
Along with them that brought their game;
This game it was, as I've heard say,
Of a black to fight with a bonny grey.

The first to come in were the Oldham lads;
They come with all the money they had;
The reason why, I heard them say,
"The black's too big for the bonny grey."

Lord Derby he come swaggering down:
"I'll lay two guineas to half a crown,
Why, if the black he gets fair play,
He'll have the wings off the bonny grey!"

And when the clock struck one, two, three,
The charcoal-black got pecked on the thigh,
They picked him up to see fair play,
But the black wouldn't fight with the bonny grey.

Cockfighting is one of the oldest spectator sports in the world, dating back 6,000 years, and was once particularly popular among the working classes. Gambling was usually involved, with bets placed and wagers attempting to predict the winner. The fighting birds, known as gamecocks, were specially bred and conditioned for elevated strength and endurance. Remnants of these special breeds still alive today are called game fowl.

# Singing Like Larks

Placed into a ring (or cockpit) with blood-thirsty onlookers gathered round, the birds were forced to fight each other. To make things worse, metal spurs were sometimes attached to the pointy natural spurs at the back of their feet. Matches often ended in death and a certain amount of physical trauma was expected or worse – desired. Advocates of this age-old sport often cite cultural and traditional reasons for its continuance, but some traditions are meant to be broken. Would they sacrifice human lives on the cold, stony altar of tradition, like the Aztecs, Vikings and many more ancient peoples before them? Unlikely.

The practice was banned outright across England and Wales in 1835, and sixty years later in Scotland, where it was relatively common in the eighteenth century. It is still popular in many countries, and no doubt still takes place illegally in the UK.

\* \* \*

Now, I know I wrote earlier in this chapter that chickens are not the most musical of birds – and I stand by it – but attempts have been made to make them so, and one of them is definitely successful.

'The Hen's March' is a tune which is at least 200 years old, with uncertain origins. I am most familiar with it being played by John Sheahan, fiddler from The Dubliners. The melody is broken up by banging fists on guitar bodies, the ends of bows hit against the tops of chin-tucked violins and chicken-like shouts from a revelling audience. It speeds up into a frenzy. Horsehairs bounce off the nylon strings in short, sharp strokes, sounding precisely like the frantic clucking and *BACAW*'ing of a chicken, which really gets the audience going.

## Chickens in the Garden

Chickens have occupied folk songs for even longer than 'The Hen's March', though. A fifteenth-century English lullaby called 'The Riddle Song' is composed of three verses, with the singer simply listing the things given to their love: a cherry with no stone, a chicken with no bone, a ring with no end and a baby with no "cryen" [crying]. A series of corresponding questions follow before the final verse, like "How can there be a cherry that has no stone?". Slow and gentle, with a whispered poignancy, the sleepy tone jars with the lyrics – words woven with lost meaning. The song name is entirely appropriate because it remains a riddle to me, ending:

> A cherry, when it's blooming, it has no stone,
> A chicken when it's pipping [hatching], it has no bone,
> A ring when it's rolling, it has no end,
> A baby when it's sleeping, has no cryen.

\* \* \*

Sneaking out in the dead of night. The tap of a rock thrown at your true love's window. Clambering up the trellis and staying until dawn. All of this is well known to a night visitor. Folk music accommodates a whole family of "night visiting songs" which all merge into one another. In these love songs, the chicken pops up in unexpected ways.

Night visiting songs are usually ended with either the man boasting about his bedroom conquest or lamenting some kind of betrayal or unrequited love. 'The Light of the Moon' breaks the mould. It has neither, ending with a cordial, though premature, parting.

Although the cockerel is not a reliable measure of time, we all know when he crows – the morning. In this song the cock crows too early and the woman, thinking it morn, shoos the man away. He is left to trudge over the cold and lonely "fallow ground" home, thinking ruefully of his love snug in bed. These two verses sum up his untimely dispatch:

Now my love she had a cock, and a pretty crowing cock,
And it crowed in the morn so very soon, so very soon.
My love, she thought it day and she hastened me away,
But it proved to be the light of the moon.

Now the cock it did crow and the wind it did blow
As I tripped o'er the plain, so very plain, so very plain.
I wished myself back in my true love's arms
And she in a bed again.

Listening to other night visiting songs, a pattern begins to emerge. Each time the cock crows, lovers are parted. Like the chiming of a clock each morning, his piercing proclamation is used to signal the passing of time. This is true even in 'The Grey Cock', an unusual ghostly song sung beautifully by Waterson–Carthy and many other famous folk musicians. Variants of the song have circulated in England since the seventeenth century, but it wasn't formally collected until 1951 by a Mrs Cecilia Costello, an Irish woman domiciling in Birmingham. In this haunting song, a lover named Willie returns from the dead but has to leave again at dawn when the cock crows. In these middle verses, as sung by Costello, the song is clearly related to 'The Light of the Moon':

"Willie dear, O dearest Willie,
Where is that colour you'd some time ago?"
"O Mary dear, the cold clay has changed me,
I am but the ghost of your Willie O."

"Then O cock, O cock, O handsome cockerel,
I pray you not crow until it's day.
For your wings I'll make of the very first beaten gold,
And your comb I'll make of the silver ray."

But the cock it crew and it crew so fully.
It crew three hours before it was day.
And before it was day my love had to go away,
Not by the light of the moon nor the light of day.

A.L. Lloyd explains in the album sleeve notes of *England &
Her Traditional Songs* (2003) that it is no ordinary chicken in
this song, but rather "a descendant of the legendary fowls of
Oriental folklore, with feathers of gold, diamond beaks and
ruby legs". In fact, the whole ballad may have been based on
ancient supernatural tales from the East.

My favourite of all the night visiting songs is "I'm a Rover",
which has a far more upbeat tune. It is a Scottish song sung in
dialect with great abandon by Luke Kelly in his live recordings:
"This is a song of love and a song of drink." Usually, the chorus
is taught to audiences beforehand and everybody sings along.
It has only a small mention of the cock, which plays precisely
the same parting role, but this time without any supernatural
significance.

I'm a Rover

*Repeated chorus:*
I'm a rover and seldom sober,
I'm a rover of high degree,
It's when I'm drinking I'm always thinking
How to gain my love's company.

# Singing Like Larks

Though the night be as dark as dungeon,
Not a star can be seen above,
I will be guided without a stumble
Into the arms of my own true love.

He stepped up to her bedroom window,
Kneeling gently upon a stone,
He whispered through her bedroom window,
"My darling dear, do you lie alone?"

She raised her head from her snow-white pillow,
Wi' her arms around her breast,
Says, "Who is that at my bedroom window
Disturbing me at my long night's rest?"

Says I, "True love, it's thy true lover,
Open the door and let me in,
For I am come on a long night's journey
More than near drenched to the skin."

She opened the door with the greatest pleasure,
She opened the door and let him in:
They both shook hands and embraced each other
Till the morning they lay as one.

The cocks were crawing, the birds were whistling,
The burns [streams] they ran free abune [above] the brae
    [hillside],
Remember, lass, I'm a ploughman laddie
And the farmer I must obey.

Now, my love, I must go and leave you
To climb the hills they are far above,
But I will climb with the greatest pleasure
Sin' I been i' the airms [arms] of my love.

148

Luke also sang another night visiting song – simply called 'The Night Visiting Song' – just one month before his untimely death in 1984, aged only forty-three. After collapsing on stage years earlier, he was diagnosed with a brain tumour and by this time was suffering with intense migraines and forgetfulness. But not for those three minutes. He knew this would be his last onstage performance, his last gaze into the crowd, and this song his self-chosen epitaph. The complicated lyrics had the rest of The Dubliners worried that he might forget the words, but Luke was determined to the last. His fingers ran nimble across a banjo as he delivered a flawlessly clear performance "without a stumble". As he finished, Ronnie Drew leant over and whispered, "Well done, Luke."

As inscribed on his gravestone, he will forever be remembered as "Luke Kelly – Dubliner".

> I must away now, I can no longer tarry,
> This morning's tempest, I have to cross,
> I must be guided, without a stumble,
> Into the arms I love the most.[18]

\* \* \*

The black-laced Andalusian, the white Burmese with striking red comb and wattle and the copper-spangled Old English Pheasant Fowl are all heritage breeds threatened by extinction. Rather than be crestfallen, the *Rare Breeds Survival Trust* has set up the Chicken Watchlist to monitor the status of British heritage breeds like the Brussbar, a well-built bird with "crele" plumage – a mixture of barred blond and gold. It only managed to cling onto existence in the 1960s by way of one breeder near Bedford.

# Singing Like Larks

Folk songs are no different. Many hang on by a single thread, perhaps in one obscure song collection, or in the mind of a single person. Many simply fade away. Just like precariously rare bird breeds, care must be taken to preserve as many traditional folk songs as possible. Singing them can do just that. If neglected, we end up with a predicament like that of 'The Haying Cock'. Bob Copper sang this song in a lost recording made by collector Peter Kennedy in 1955. That is all I or anyone knows – except for the first line: "One morning, oh so early, on the feast of Valentine..."

I wonder if (and hope that) someone, somewhere knows 'The Haying Cock'. Its title teases us like a tuneful, misplaced relic, so near yet so far. What melody is it sung to? What story lies within? Perhaps, as you read this, the title rings the tiniest bell in the corner of the forgetful mind, or flutters the yellowing note tucked into a dusty book with the lyrics scribbled down, momentarily illuminated by the faint remembrance. One day it might flourish again but, for now, we are left with a title, a line – a vague rumour of a song that once lived.

# If I Were a Blackbird...

## (*Turdus merula*)

*Now summer it is coming, what pleasure we shall see,*
*The small birds are a-singing on every green tree,*
*The blackbirds and the thrushes are a-whistling merrilie.*

– 'The Jolly Waggoner'

A COLLY BIRD. A coaly bird. With a body black as obsidian, their glassy eyes pop like glaring embers. Their matching fiery bill highlights the air like a waving sparkler at night, curiously darting in and out of hedgy cover. They are a substantial bird, just large enough to command your full attention. With mottled breast and throat, both male and (confusingly) nut-brown female "blackbirds" are amiable souls, tamed by constant human interaction. They are not afraid to face you dead on, before turning their heads left and right, looking at you with one eye, then the other, working out what you are and – more pressingly – what you have to offer.

# Singing Like Larks

The blackbird is a "true thrush", the name given to medium-sized birds in the genus *Turdus* of the wider thrush family, *Turdidae*. It is difficult to mistake a blackbird for another type of thrush. As far as the male is concerned, the *Catchphrase* motto seems applicable: "say what you see". However, just by listening alone, it can be tricky to thrash out the different thrushes.

Bookending the day with music, at dawn and dusk (and at night under street lighting), the blackbird and creamy white, buff-speckled song thrush sound flutily similar. But there are slight differences. The blackbird sounds mellower and more controlled, whilst the song thrush changes pitch anxiously, as if it feels the pressure of having "song" in its name.

Apart from their similar voices, I wonder why they are almost always paired together in folk music. When the following traditional songs refer to the "thrush", I assume they mean the song thrush, which is roughly five times more populous than the larger and bolder mistle thrush. The latter slurs and rattles drunkenly in all weathers, living up to its old name of "stormcock". The blackbird is more populous than both, being the only UK thrush that is not RSPB red-listed. In fact, the blackbird is recorded more than any other bird in the Roud Folk Song Index by some margin – 611 records, followed by the nightingale's 570!

### Blackbirds and Thrushes
As I was a-walking for my recreation,
Down by the green meadows I silently strayed.
There I met a fair maid making great lamentation,
"Oh, Jimmy will be slain in the wars I'm afraid."

# If I Were a Blackbird

The blackbirds and thrushes sing in the green bushes,
The larks and the doves seem to mourn for this maid.
And the song she sang was concerning her lover;
"Oh, Jimmy will be slain in the wars I'm afraid."

When Jimmy returned with his heart full of yearning,
He found his dear Mary all dead in her grave.
He cried, "I'm forsaken, my poor heart is breaking,
I wish that I never had left this fair maid."

This *Romeo & Juliet*-esque traditional song holds blackbirds and thrushes at the very centre. Blackbirds are monogamous, sticking with one partner until death. A true thrush indeed. I have certainly always imagined them a loyal bird, guiding us through backroads and byways. They are abundant on one of my regular local walks that I take whenever I get some time to myself: through a small wood, across a rickety wooden-planked bridge, down a narrow footpath bordered by grazing horses, fenced with barbed wire. The footpath leads into another copse, chiming with the repetitive see-saw call of the great tit, and finally gives way to a rolling expanse of winter crops. I had never ventured any further until, one day, I had some company.

A sandy path winds up to my left. It leads up a steep hill (steep by Essex standards, at least) where a line of ancient, deep-rooted oaks waymark the hilltop like an island causeway. They appear unaffected by the cumulative storms that seem to keep on battering us, wave after wave. Just then a female blackbird pops out of the gnarled hawthorn hedge bordering the path, gazing up at me from the scattered shards of bark.

At the top of the hill is a Grade II listed private hall, dating to 1199 – our arbitrary destination, the blackbird's and mine. Like a paid tour, the blackbird escorts me all the way, tripling through the skeletal trees and skipping from hedge to path and back again. I follow in her wake. High-rise flats appear in the distance as we climb this bare landscape and, reaching the red-brick hall, the opening through which I had entered the field now looks only large enough for a field mouse to squeeze through.

The blackbird and I earnt a lofty viewpoint uncommon in this relatively flat county. It felt like freedom.

> One evening as I walked down by yon green bush
> I heard two birds whistling; the blackbird and thrush,
> I asked them the reason why they were so merry,
> The answer they gave me: They were single and free.[19]

\* \* \*

'Blackbirds and Thrushes' has two things in common with a song called 'Hares on the Mountain':

They are both sung by Shirley Collins MBE, now in her late eighties.

They were both collected by Cecil Sharp (1859-1924) – a composer and collector of thousands of songs from rural England during the first folk song revival.

Shirley, from Hastings in Sussex, is the First Lady of folk. She is acclaimed for her high-pitched and austere singing style, delivering each line without unnecessary ornamentation or inflection. She tells the story of a song without distractions. Cecil Sharp published 'Hares on the Mountain' in *Folk Songs from Somerset* (1904), and Shirley recorded this in her 1958 album *Sweet England* when she was only twenty-two years old, accompanied by a banjo:

Hares on the Mountain
If all you young men were hares on the mountain,
How many young girls would take guns and go hunting?
With a ri-fol-de-di, cal-ol-de-day, ri-fol-ai-de.

If the young men could sing like blackbirds and thrushes,
How many young girls would go beating the bushes?
With a ri-fol-de-di, cal-ol-de-day, ri-fol-ai-de.

If all you young men were rushes a-growing,
How many young girls would take scythes and go mowing?
With a ri-fol-de-di, cal-ol-de-day, ri-fol-ai-de.

If all you young men were ducks in the water,
How many young girls would undress and dive after?
With a ri-fol-de-di, cal-ol-de-day, ri-fol-ai-de.

But the young men are given to frisking and fooling,
I'll leave them alone and attend to my schooling
With a ri-fol-de-di, cal-ol-de-day, ri-fol-ai-de.

This daydream of a song turns traditional courtship on its head with the women in pursuit of the men. It is sung to tunes both slow and fast, and its popularity amongst folk singers has borne many different versions.

Although he never recorded it, 'Hares on the Mountain' reminds me of one of the last genuine British source singers[20]: Sam Larner (1878-1965), a Norfolk herring fisherman, who kept alive many songs of the sea – those with plenty of salt in them. He liked the girls, and in his younger days, he could always get one. "A fresh one in every port," he said, declaring at the end of one of his records, "I've been a lil' bit naughty in my time, but no 'arm, no 'arm."

# Singing Like Larks

\* \* \*

HAUL!
"Windy old weather, stormy old weather,
When the wind blows we'll all pull together."[21]
HAUL!

Do fishermen sing nowadays? Sea shanties were once sung by fishermen to keep everyone in time as they hauled in the nets, not just by Fisherman's Friends today. Singing also raised morale and kept men lively whilst out on watch, battling against the rockabye waves attempting to lull them back to sleep. With the rest of the crew snug in their cabins, no cloud cover for insulation and the rigging as sole witness to the complete isolation, one had to pass the time somehow.

It used to be said that "They were all singers at Winterton" and Sam Larner was foremost among them. Over a third of the 800 residents in this north-Norfolk village were fishermen – including Sam's father – so a life at sea seemed inevitable. "Why, for me and my brothers it was either sea or gaol [jail], and that for my sisters that was service or gaol," Sam explains to BBC's Charles Parker in a 1962 home interview for a programme called *The Singer and the Song*. By this time he was in his late eighties, wrinkled and half deaf, but his one good eye still sparkled at the sight of a pretty girl.

Whilst growing up, Sam learnt old songs from his grandfather and locals in the pub, earning pennies by singing them to visiting coach parties. "I soon picked up the old songs. The ruder they were the quicker I picked 'em up!" There was no cinema, and little to entertain a young man except for the train into Great Yarmouth so, in 1892 aged only thirteen, Sam first went to sea.

Oh, it was a fine and a pleasant day,
Out of Yarmouth harbour I was faring
As a cabin boy on a sailing lugger,
For to hunt the bonny shoals of herring.

This is a verse from 'The Shoals of Herring', a song written by Ewan MacColl following a fisherman's progress from cabin boy to deckhand. It was inspired by Sam's seafaring life, singing the fishing.[22]

Life as the youngest and lowest-ranked crew member was tough. Sam recalls the dread of going to sea for the first time: you'd be "on the knucklebones of your arse". Some of the older fishermen "didn't care for nothing … cruel old men. You weren't allowed to speak" and if you were sleepy they would "chuck a bucket of water on you". He was given the most dangerous jobs, such as climbing the rigging to trim the sails or stowing the top-sail, and for twenty long weeks in the North Sea, his reward was a mere five pounds. "We were poor as church mice. That's 'ow it was that time o' day, yesss," he tells interviewer Charles.

In 1894, Sam signed as a deckhand on *The Snowflake*, another sailing vessel. He learnt on the job, continuing to soak up songs from his crewmates like a sponge and began frequenting singing and step dancing pub sessions. "I've sung in every port in the British Isles," he says.

Sam explains to Charles that, "We'd go down to Shetlands, then up as far as Shields, then have a touch at Scarborough, then down to Grimsby for the 'ome fishing[23] up Christmas." In 1907, Sam even won a singing competition in Lerwick on the Shetland Islands. "I got the most encore of the whole lot … they wouldn't let me sit down; I had to sing them another song!" he says. "These people all know about it here; I aren't tellin' stories. And I got the first prize." Sam's energy and manner of speaking captivated an audience and if youngsters were too noisy in the pub when he was singing, they were thrown out.

Forgotten words stunt the conversation with Charles as he has to ask after their meaning: words picked up over a lifetime at sea like a "shimmer", equating to a hundred "cran" of herring. In a smart shirt and jacket, he excitedly boxes the compass (meaning to quickly recite the compass points in correct order) and reels off stories, sealore and rhymes once taught to young sailors to help with navigation:

*"When in danger or in doubt, always keep a sharp look out. If you 'aven't got room to turn, ease her, stop her or go astern. If on your starboard red appear, it is your duty to keep clear, to act as judgment says is proper, ease her, back her or stop her."*

*"Quick rise, after low, indicates the stronger blow. Long foretold, long last, short notice, soon past."*

Sam falls silent, scans the faces in the room, leans forward in his armchair and builds the anticipation of the song to come by asking: "Are you ready for it? Would you like to have it?" Each line is made special as he acts out the lyrics with his hands and chuckles through some of the words. Such rare digital treasures allow us to run aground on these faraway moments; we can imagine wooden fishing boats and sails flapping in a distant but altogether familiar wind.

Working his way up the ranks and experiencing first-hand the shift from sail to steam, Sam fished until 1933 when, at age fifty-six, he could fish no longer due to abdominal strain from decades of pulling heavy nets.

In this world of salt and sails, I would not have expected the blackbird or the thrush to be netted in one of Sam's songs. But, in 'Pleasant and Delightful' – thought to have its origins in the early seventeenth century – there they are, accompanied by a customary midsummer lark.

### Pleasant and Delightful

It was pleasant and delightful one midsummer's morn,
When the green fields and meadows were buried in corn,
And the blackbirds and thrushes sang on every green tree,
[And the larks they sang melodious]²⁴ at the dawn of the day.

Said the sailor to his true love, "I am bound far away,
I am bound for the East Indies, where the loud cannons roar.
I am bound for the East Indies, where the loud cannons roar,
[I am going to leave my Nancy], she's the girl I adore."

Said the sailor to his true love, "I no longer can stay,
For her topsails are hoisted and the anchor is weighed.
Our ship she lays waiting for the next flowing tide.
[And if ever I return again] I will make you my bride."

A ring from her finger she then instantly drew,
Saying, "Take this, dearest William, and my heart shall go, too."
And while he embraced her tears from her eyes fell,
[Saying, "May I go along with you?"] "Oh no, me love, farewell."

Blackbirds and larks, both front-row dawn chorists, play the scene-setting role here for poor William and Nancy. What I love best about Sam's recording of 'Pleasant and Delightful' is what he says after the song, granting an insight into life at sea for a newly married man:

*When you come 'ome, you might have been away seven or eight weeks down on the North Sea, ho, that's when that used to be lovely. About when I first got married, you know, I'd long to get home then. I used to count the days and then, you know, you began to feel trilly – you know – frilty!*

*★Raspy laughter★*

*It was like getting fresh married again when you'd been away for about ten or a dozen weeks. Lovely. Oh, that's all gone for me now and that's the reason I don't care if I live or die.*

It was 1956, in a smoky pub, when a BBC Birmingham radio producer called Phillip Donnellan met Sam by chance. Phillip happened to be searching for working people to provide him with old songs and information about the past. With a repertoire of over sixty traditional songs, he got more than he bargained for with Sam.

Phillip brought Sam to the attention of Ewan MacColl and Peggy Seeger who asked him to perform in the Ballads and Blues Club in London where MacColl recalls that "Sam sat and sang and talked to several hundred young people who hung on his every word and gesture as though he had been Ulysses newly returned from Troy to Ithaca. He never forgot it." With their help, Sam managed to release an LP in 1961 containing nineteen tracks of singing and talking about his life and the fishing industry. Sam ended his days as "the star of East Anglian folk singing" and is considered one of the most important traditional singers of the twentieth century. He may have passed on in 1965, but Sam's natural charisma, rich turn of phrase and love of the old songs floats buoyantly in his recordings for all to hear.

\* \* \*

# If I Were a Blackbird

Wintertime in Winterton. That is when I visited Sam's small semi-detached cottage by the tall, square and flint-encrusted church. It is a holiday home now, with little to mark it out apart from a blue plaque on the wall: "Sam Larner, 1878–1965, Fisherman & Folk Singer". It was dead quiet – the cold made sure of that – but the local shop still provided tea and a sausage roll. Walking to where the street gives way to sand, the sea appeared over the dunes. I half expected to see some fishing boats scattered at sea, but an undisturbed horizon lay before me.

A colony of Atlantic grey seals were hauled up on the beach, pupping season. The sand looked well salted and peppered, with the adults' dark fur contrasting with the white, fluffy pups. This collection of barking, honking, roaring sea dogs wriggled around, some curved like kidney beans on their sides, others nose-to-nose. Many were occupied with evading the incoming tide, clumsily dragging themselves to safety like fish out of water.

On the walk back, I was parallel with furrowed fields on both sides. Something picked around in my peripheral. I turned and raised my binoculars to see a dozen or so stocky fieldfares. Their rusty yellow breasts glowed against the soaking earth and their black spots shone like scales in the low sun. As they stood nobly upright, I could see why the Spanish call them the "royal thrush". Watching them reminded me of the blackbird in 'Pleasant and Delightful', and I hummed the tune in honour of this bird's colourful cousin.

As I approached the car, I wondered if the moulting seal pups were daydreaming about the day when they would head out to sea for the first time, joining the hunt for herring and other seafood delights, like Sam did long ago. After all, as the title of his LP attests, *Now is the Time for Fishing*.

# Singing Like Larks

\* \* \*

As the sun set on the age of sail and steamships took over, the minimum school leaving age was ever-increasing. It was ten years old in 1880, eleven in 1893 and thirteen by the end of 1899 – getting better, but still nowhere near old enough for a full education.

For the short time children spent in school, nursery rhymes played an important teaching role. They still help young children today to develop storytelling and language skills, practising rhythm and song patterns whilst reciting them. The catchy tunes capture a certain imaginative wonder, unbound by the ties of reality. Cows jump over the moon, dishes run away with the spoon. Well-known nursery rhymes like 'Jack and Jill', 'Three Blind Mice', and 'Humpty Dumpty' all seem to exist within this same immersive, strange, parallel reality.

Whilst wondrous and magical, I cannot help but find nursery rhymes slightly creepy. They fall into the "uncanny valley" where the world represented in them is like our own, but slightly removed. There is something vaguely "off" about them. The role of a young child is to soak up knowledge and try to navigate what is real and what is not, but these rhymes blur the line. Nursery rhymes are not exactly "childish", filled with death, illness, falls, breaks, fallen bridges, falling cradles – the list goes on. An unstable, dangerous world lies within where disaster lurks around each corner, and everything seems liable to fall. Perhaps these didactic tales of warning are a necessary first encounter with the darker side of life, preparing children for the real world.

A feeling also arises that many of these old rhymes are based in more than just fiction. Some were written in protest, others for propaganda and many were inspired by actual historical events, which gives them a lasting depth, pulling them from one generation to the next.

Exactly what makes nursery rhymes so memorable? Folklorists have been trying to find out for years.

'Sing a Song of Sixpence' is a classic. It hosts "four and twenty blackbirds", and little Jenny Wren:

### Sing a Song of Sixpence

Sing a song of sixpence,
A pocket full of rye.
Four and twenty blackbirds,
Baked in a pie.

When the pie was opened
The birds began to sing;
Wasn't that a dainty dish,
To set before the king?

The king was in his counting house,
Counting out his money;
The queen was in the parlour,
Eating bread and honey.

The maid was in the garden,
Hanging out the clothes,
When down came a blackbird
And pecked off her nose.

And shortly after that,
There came a little wren,
As she sat upon a chair,
And put it on again.

As expected, the origins are unknown, but the first printed version of this rhyme appears in *Tommy Thumb's Pretty Song*

*Book*, published in London around 1744. There was a time, around the sixteenth century, when live birds were placed in pies for simple amusement. An Italian cookbook from 1549 contains a recipe which provides instructions regarding how "to make pies so that birds may be alive in them and fly out when it is cut up". Sitting down and digging in, what a spectacle it must have been to see songbirds fly out!

It has been suggested that the "four and twenty blackbirds" symbolise the twenty-four hours in the day, with the queen representing the moon and the king representing the sun. Others have more gravely perceived the nose-stealing blackbird as a demon stealing the maid's soul! This evil portrayal is par for the course for any dark-coloured bird. If the blackbird is the demon in this scenario, then the restorative wren must surely be the angel.

\* \* \*

The Blackbird of Sweet Avondale
By the bright bay of Dublin, while carelessly strolling,
I sat myself down by a clear crystal shade.
Reclined on the beach, as the wild waves were rolling,
In sorrow condoling, I spied a fair maid.

Her hopes changed to mourning, that once were so glorious.
I sat in amazement to hear her sad tale.
Her heartstrings burst forth in wild accents deploring,
Saying, "Where is my blackbird of sweet Avondale?"

"Through the counties of Wicklow, Kerry, Cork and Tipperary,
The praises of Ireland, my blackbird did sing.
But woe to the hour, when with heart light and airy,
That heaved from my arms, to Dublin took wing."

# If I Were a Blackbird

"All the birds in the forest their notes there to cheer me.
Not even the song of the sweet nightingale.
Her notes so encharming fills my heart with alarm,
Since I lost my blackbird of sweet Avondale."

"Oh the peelers waylaid him in hopes to ensnare him,
While I here in sorrow, his absence bewail.
It grieves me to think that the walls of Kilmainham
Surrounds my poor blackbird of sweet Avondale."

"Oh, Erin, my country, awake from your slumbers.
And bring back my blackbird, so dear unto me.
And let everyone see, by the strength of your numbers,
That Ireland, a nation, would like to be free."

'The Blackbird of Sweet Avondale' was actually the nickname given to Irish nationalist politician Charles Stewart Parnell (1846-1891) after his birthplace – Avondale in Co. Wicklow. He campaigned for Irish Home Rule and was incarcerated in Kilmainham Gaol, Dublin, until he renounced violent extra-parliamentary action. It is not unusual in Irish history for a leader to be nicknamed after a bird. 'The Green Linnet' is a broadside ballad about Napoleon. The first verse goes like this:

Curiosity led a young native of Erin
To view the lone banks of the Rhine
Where an empress he saw and the robe that she was wearing
All over with diamonds did shine.
No goddess in splendour was ever yet seen
To equal this fair maid so mild and serene
In soft murmurs she cried, "Oh, my linnet so green
Sweet Boney, will I ne'er see you more?"

# Singing Like Larks

Just a twenty-minute drive from Avondale is Glendalough, which has its own links to the blackbird. The name brings forth my own memories of annual summertime visits to see family on the Wicklow-Kildare border.

Glendalough is a sixth-century monastic settlement, built in the trough of a wide U-shaped valley within the Wicklow Mountains, which was carved out during the last ice age by a bulldozing glacier. Emerald green runs up the valley sides, intruded by bare outcrops of striated rock where the gradient becomes too severe for the greenery to cling on. Heather presents the hills with dramatic darkness and pines scent the air. Every colour appears enhanced, saturated.

The view, filled with health and abundance, is interrupted by dull grave slabs, leaning forward and back, reminding passers-by of their impermanence. Still, even these are painted with yellow lichen. Various sacred buildings stand in ruin, their slate roofs long gone, revealing the floor to the sky. Granite blocks of different dimensions form distinctly Celtic walls, windows and decorative arches. Stone surfaces are iced like a birthday cake with a thick layer of moss. Two buildings remain intact, a tall and thin round tower, pointed at the top, which looks as if Rapunzel is about to throw down her hair, and St Kevin's Kitchen, which is a nave-and-chancel church from the twelfth century, with a small bell tower resembling a chimney.

The low sun peeping over the mountains sparkles off the mica in the round tower, matching the colours of autumn and casting a long shadow across the valley – a shining gold beacon signalling that all of life's treasures exist here. St Kevin, the founder of the monastic city, knew this to be true, creating workshops, guest houses, an infirmary, farm buildings and dwellings for both monks and a large lay population. Today, the uncountable years of prayer and self-reflection, as well as a history of raids and destruction, has forged a palpable spirituality which drives pilgrims to think contemplatively about life's big questions.

St Kevin died in 618 A.D., but not before mastering meditation and reflection in his final spring. The story goes that, one day, he was deep in prayer with his eyes closed and one upturned palm outstretched "stiff as a crossbeam"[25] out of the church window. He stayed silent and still for so long that a blackbird flew down, built a nest in his hand and laid an egg in it. As he remained motionless, the egg eventually hatched, and St Kevin has been the patron saint of the blackbird ever since.

\* \* \*

From Ireland's shores we catch a ferry to the heart of agricultural southern England to find 'Three Maidens to Milking Did Go'. Collected by various people and in various places, Bob Copper discovered this traditional song whilst song collecting around Sussex and Hampshire for the BBC during the 1950s.

He recalls that the weather was unusually hot. Reaching the small Hampshire town of Mapledurwell (meaning "Maple Tree Spring") by six p.m., he heard from the locals that a man called Fred Hewett – known as "Gran'fer" – was a lover of the old songs. Directed to the fields, Bob found the old man of over seventy still working, "ploughing a ten-acre piece of fallow two fields back from the road".[26] Fred was driving an "old Fordson tractor with sagging axles back and forth across the field turning the rich, dark loam up into corduroy ridges". Quite a change from the pair of heavy horses that Fred would have followed in his youth, but he was of the generation who experienced the transition from muscle and horse power to machines.

A thrush sang in the hedgerow and a bumblebee was inspecting each mauve foxglove beside Bob, who was absorbing the "earth's prevailing mood": a deep calm, shattered only by the tractor engine. Presently, Fred finished his work, hitched off the plough and drove to the gateway where his audience of one waited. Shouting over the tractor noise, Bob explained his musical mission to which Fred replied, "Follow me." Back at his home of Spring Cottages, he removed his mud-caked boots at the back doorstep, slipped his braces from his shoulders, leaving only his "stout leather belt" to hold his armpit-high corduroys, and stood there in his socks, singing with a forehead still damp from work:

Three Maidens to Milking Did Go
Three maidens to milking did go,
Three maidens to milking did go.
And the wind it did blow high and the wind it did blow low,
And it tossed milking pails to and fro.

I met with a man I knew well,
And I kindly asked of him if he had got any skills
For to catch me a small bird or two.

"Oh, yes, I got some excellent good skills.
Now, come along with me down to yonder shady tree.
I'll catch thee a small bird or two."

Here's luck to the blackbird and thrush,
There's luck to the blackbird and thrush.
It's a bird of one feather and we'll all flock together,
Let the people say little or much.

# If I Were a Blackbird

Here's luck to the jolly dragoon.
Here's luck to the jolly dragoon.
We'll ramble all the day and at night we'll spend or play,
And go home by the light of the moon.

What was the result of travelling around collecting songs from the horse's mouth, as it were? The very genuine article. You can hear Fred sing this song on a 1977 Topic Records LP called *Songs and Southern Breezes* which is composed of Bob's recordings taken on his travels.

This piece of countryside quaintness has been plastered with sexual innuendo by folk song experts and enthusiasts. Bob did not dwell on such interpretations (thinking it took away the magic) and Fred later confirmed that he saw no innuendo, accepting it at face value as "a very good song". Other fuller versions, sometimes called 'The Bird in the Bush', tell of a young man meeting a trio of girls, going with them into the woods where the leaves are thickest and engaging in a sociable act. A. L. Lloyd considered Fred's rendition to be a bowdlerisation of one of the most sensual folk songs in existence.

In protest, Bob writes:

*Whether the songs were written intentionally with double meanings I know not, nor am I expert enough to guess. But I do think that many present-day students of traditional songs, with their urbane and sophisticated need of excitement, too readily read into them meanings that certainly never entered the heads of the old singers. Almost without exception I found that the old singers were entirely innocent of any hidden significance in the words they were singing and, in fact, were rather shocked when the possibility was put to them. Then it was I, and not the song, that was suspect for even suggesting it.*

# Singing Like Larks

When Bob Copper was due to set out on his song-collecting travels for the BBC, he knew that he would need a car. He bought a 1932 Morris Major from a friend for twenty-five pounds, complete with wire wheels and a sunroof stuck closed which "admitted more rain than sunshine". The door handles were fastened with binder-twine (as was the fanbelt on the way to Mapledurwell) and the paintwork was patchy, which gave the motor a homely, rustic feel. This was to prove advantageous for the work he was about to embark upon.

In recording the older generation of countrymen and women – who may never have even used a telephone – Bob's success depended greatly upon trust. He had to win it and get his subjects thoroughly relaxed and in their natural state before pulling out the strange recording contraption and inviting them to sing. Pints of beer and pipes of tobacco went a long way, but he found that his own appearance and experience helped him greatly.

On one visit to a small hamlet called Axford, the news got around the local Crown pub that "a chap from the BBC" was coming to visit – this caused quite a stir. Many must have expected a city mouse in a pinstripe suit to appear from a limousine. What they got was a fellow man of the soil, of country origins and upbringing, turning up in "the Major". The town breathed a common sigh of relief. "Oh, I'm glad it turned out to be a man o' no consequence," said Enos White to Bob in the pub that evening. He was a fellow folk singer and also Fred's brother-in-law. "To 'ear 'em talking 'ere las' night you would've thought we wuz going to meet the Queen or somewhat."

* * *

## If I Were a Blackbird

Bob Copper spent many summer holidays as a boy helping out on the farm in Rottingdean and understood the jobs that needed to be done at harvest time and at other times of year. One of these was bird scaring. When farmers plant crops in the springtime, crows especially will come down and eat the seeds. Like human scarecrows, children would be sent into the fields with clappers – a plank of wood with a handle and two other bits of wood tied on so that swinging it back and forth made a series of air-splitting CRACKS. An age-old battle between birds and farmers continues today and is evident in agricultural folk songs.

> Where be yon blackbird to?
> I know where 'e be!
> 'E be up yon wurzel tree
> An' I be a'ter 'e!
> Well, 'e sees I, an' I sees 'e,
> An' 'e knows I be a'ter 'e,
> With a bloody great stick, an' 'alf a brick
> An' blackbird, I'll 'ave 'e![27]

The crow *is* a black bird, but not a blackbird. Nor is a blackbird a crow. This dialectic song from Somerset likely refers to the crow, a notorious arable field plunderer, although blackbirds will eat grains and seeds too. As unfussy omnivores, blackbirds can often be seen scanning the ground for food, bursting into short sprints between tasty morsels with their heads pushed forwards like a photo finish on race day.

A similar song which likely also means to condemn the crow rather than the blackbird is 'I Know Where There's a Blackbird's Nest'. It has not been well collected but was documented in 1964 from Mr Cantwell in Oxfordshire.

# Singing Like Larks

## I Know Where There's a Blackbird's Nest[28]

I know where there's a blackbird's nest
I know where 'e be
'E be in yon turnip field, and I be after 'e
'E spies I and I spies 'e,
He calls I a bu**er and a liar
When I find that blackbird's nest
I'll set the bu**er on fire.

Working on a farm, four and twenty years
'E can't take the rise out of I
For there ain't no bird on this y'ere farm
Can hide his nest from I.

I wish I was back home in Gloucester
Where all them birds they flock round I
I'd clap my hands and laugh like bu**ery
*Laughs* Just to see them blackbirds fly.

Be I Somerset, be I bu**ery
I comes up from Wareham.
Me mother's got ten more like I
Because she knows how to rare 'em,
And they calls I Buttercup Joe.

*Spoken*: That's it!

When diaphanous blankets of snow melt away to clear space for a galaxy of wood anemones which light the woodland floor, a drizzly day will come in March when the male blackbirds all warble together. Wood and vale will swell with song like fresh rosebuds from dawn to dimness. "Where be yon blackbird to?" Hear them throughout the spring, with each fresh bloom, and after summer rains when many other birds have fallen silent.

# If I Were a Blackbird

\* \* \*

It seems fitting as we near the end of this chapter of land and sea to row out one last time with a traditional English sea song known by almost every collector. It was first collected in May 1906 from Mr Henry Lee in Whitchurch, Hampshire:

### If I Was a Blackbird

I am a poor girl and my fortune seems sad,
Six months have I courted a true sailor lad;
And truly I loved him by night and by day
And now in his transport he's sailed far away.

*Chorus:*
If I was a blackbird, could whistle and sing,
I'd follow the vessel my true love sails in;
And on the top rigging there I'd build my nest
And lay down all night on his lily-white breast.

My love's tall and handsome in every degree,
His parents despise him because he loved me;
But let them despise him and say what they will,
While I've breath in my body I'll love him still.

He promised he'd meet me at Bonnybrook Fair
With a bunch of blue ribbons to tie up my hair;
And if he would meet me I'd crown him with joy,
And kiss those fond lips of my dear sailor boy.

If I was a scholar, could handle my pen,
Just one private letter to him I would send.
I'd write and I'd tell him of my grief and woe
And far o'er the oceans with my true love I'd go.

# Singing Like Larks

Most of us have looked to the sky and wondered what it would be like to fly. To outstretch our wings and kick off from the ground, struggling upwards in search of a quiet perch. Looking onto rooftops and patchwork fields seems like a peaceful existence – heavy worries and grief left below. Maybe the reason why blackbirds are included in so many folk songs is because they remind us of what it means to be free. Like the romantic waggoner in this final song, driving his horse from village to village bearing goods, let us sing alongside them.

## The Jolly Waggoner
When first I went a-waggoning, a-waggoning did go,
I filled my poor old parents' hearts with sorrow, grief and woe.
And many are the hardships that since I've undergone.

*Chorus:*
Sing wo, me lads, sing wo!
Drive on, me lads, drive on!
Who wouldn't be for all the world a jolly waggoner?

Well it's pelting down with rain, me lads, I'm wet unto the skin,
I will bear it with a contented heart until I reach the inn
And then I'll get a drinking with the landlord and his kin.

Now summer it is coming, what pleasure we shall see,
The small birds are a-singing on every green tree,
The blackbirds and the thrushes are a-whistling merrilie.

Now Michaelmas is coming, what pleasure we shall find,
It will make the gold to fly, my boys, like chaff before the wind,
And every lad shall take his lass, so loving and so kind.

# Be More Owl

## (*Strigiformes*)

*Of all the birds that ever I see,*
*The owl is the fairest in her degree*

– 'Of All the Birds'

KN – *OWL* – EDGE. By definition, all six owl species found in the UK are very knowledgeable – born with highly advanced tools designed for gathering information from their surroundings. From short to long-eared, tawny to barn, they slip silently through the air like grace in motion so as not to disrupt their intense listening. Millions of years of aeronautic evolutionary engineering has freed the owl from having to hear over itself.

The owl's wide face acts like those concave World War II-era sound mirrors dotted around Britain in the days before radar. However, the owl listens for its prey, not for German aircraft across the Channel. Flying over open fields at night, they map the sounds on the ground like a surveying vessel bouncing sonar off the sea floor, building up a picture of what lies below. A downward-facing beak and stiff ring of feathers around the face (like the lip of a plate) channel sound to the ear holes to maximise the owl's listening ability, just as we might cup our hands behind our ears to hear more effectively – or to perform an orangutang impression.

At certain frequencies, the owl's hearing is ten times more sensitive than our own. In the spirit of fair play, one might think that evolution would leave it there. Acute hearing is surely enough to survive. And yet, owls also possess laser-like vision, helping to form one of the most well-equipped killing machines on Earth.

\* \* \*

Imagine the Outer Hebrides in the gloaming[29] when the nights are drawing in. A short-eared owl perches on a farmer's gate. Sulphur-yellow eyes, ear tufts tucked back and a permanently irritable expression. Every so often, the bird mechanically swivels its streaky brown head a full 270 degrees to look behind itself like a jack-knifed artic. One half expects to hear the clicks of cogs working inside. Scanning … watching … probing. Stop. The creature recoils its head to propel its sights deeper into a distant hedgerow. Then it slips silently off the gate and stays low across a meadow. Moving fast and erratically, it fans the darkening air like a behe–*moth*.

A field mouse scampers and scurries through an enmeshed realm of knee-high heather and rough grass, feeding on fallen seeds. Its whiskers twitch and swish past blades of grass. Its gnawing is audible to owl ears. Homing in on the twilight disturbance, the predator swoops down for a silent assault and deadly display of audial and visual supremacy. Just before it reaches the unsuspecting quarry, the owl unfurls its wings and swings its eight talons in front, landing with a razor-sharp bump into fur and flesh. No celebration required. The owl expects to make the catch. It seems as if the outcome was guaranteed the moment it set eyes on its furry foe. Looks cannot kill but, for the little brown mouse, the end came quick.

In my mind, no other creature serves as a greater reminder of how much of the world we miss than the owl. Limited hearing. Limited vision. Only a tiny sliver of the world is accessible to us. That other world of mile-long distance, the beat of a beetle's wings and paddy paw-steps across muddy ground passes us by. We negotiate the world as moles, seeing only what is right in front of us. Even then we lack a mole's "stereo" sense of smell as they use their brush-like noses to paint the world around them into a full olfactory picture. Humans are incredibly intelligent but are sensorily outmatched by our natural peers. Knowledge is one thing but accepting that fact is surely wisdom.

\* \* \*

*"Owl is the grand and rather clever old man of the forest"*

– A.A. Milne

You have probably heard the phrase "wise old owl" and, whilst Owl – the stuffy and talkative character in *Winnie-the-Pooh* – is not as wise as he thinks he is (spelling his name "WOL" and living in "The Wolery"), this order of birds has been celebrated as such since time immemorial.

### A Wise Old Owl
There was an old owl liv'd in an oak
The more he heard, the less he spoke,

# Singing Like Larks

The less he spoke, the more he heard.
O, if men were like that wise old bird.

A version of this nursery rhyme was first published in *Punch*, April 10, 1875 – a British weekly satirical magazine printed from 1841 to 2002. The author is unknown, but it was based on an older traditional nursery rhyme beginning "There was an owl lived in an oak, wisky, wasky, weedle". A later version of 'A Wise Old Owl' was employed during World War II by the US army who tweaked the ending to "Soldier ... be like that old bird!" with the caption "Silence means security". It was intended to encourage servicemen and citizens alike to beware of unguarded talk that could undermine the war effort. The closest equivalent I have heard is "Loose lips sink ships" but I prefer the owl version.

Owls have been assigned the virtue of wisdom at least since the time of ancient Greece. Athena – the beautiful goddess of battle strategy and wisdom – is traditionally accompanied by a little owl and today her name is used for a genus of nine owl species called *Athene*, including the little owl (*Athene noctua*), which is resident in Britain. But why are owls perceived as wise? Their large, all-seeing eyes and solemn appearance likely play a role. If eyes are the window to the soul then owls look out of grand, stained glass windows. Just like crepuscular (active during dawn and dusk) and nocturnal owls can see through the darkness, Goddess Athena is said to be able to "see" when others cannot, but in a less literal sense – by staying calm and gaining insights which go over the heads of us mere mortals.

The owl's attraction to aged things also adds to this image of wisdom, as they choose to roost in the holes of ancient, sturdy trees, ruinous buildings and tumbledown barns. As alluded to in 'A Wise Old Owl', their mastery of silence also grants them a reserved and even judgemental quality, resulting in wise and – in the case of A.A. Milne's Owl – supercilious artistic portrayals.

I am reminded of a section in F. Scott Fitzgerald's *The Great Gatsby* when the narrator, Nick Carraway, slips away into Gatsby's oak-panelled Gothic library to escape an over-whelmingly lavish house party. Gatsby, the mysterious host, is nowhere to be found, but sitting at the end of a huge table is a stout, middle-aged, bespectacled man referred to as "Owl Eyes". He is just another partygoer but comes to symbolise per-ception and insight. The reason for Gatsby's party is unclear, and his gargantuan library is suspected to be a folly, mere the-atre, like the pastel-coloured house fronts in Portmeirion. Owl Eyes is shocked to discover that all of the books are real:

> *"Absolutely real – have pages and everything. I thought they'd be a nice durable cardboard. Matter of fact, they're absolutely real. Pages and – Here! Lemme show you."*

Apart from the narrator, the end of the novel reveals that old Owl Eyes is one of the only characters perceptive enough to see through the façade to understand Gatsby's true human-ity. When the parties end, every single greedy guest deserts Gatsby, but not him.

The folk traditions of other countries also present the same wise themes, like '*Sowa*' ('Owl'), a traditional Polish song which is delivered in chilling emotive harmony. It sounds tribal, like something you might expect to hear had you stumbled across a fire circle in the wilderness:

# Singing Like Larks

An owl sits in the barn,
And listens who talks with whom.
Here's day, day, there's night, night,
Here's poverty, there's desire, desire,
And listens who talks with whom.[30]

These species undoubtedly play a cross-cultural role as the sagacious spectre, the erudite elder and the ornithological observer. If birds collected folk songs, the owl would have the broadest repertoire of them all.

* * *

My closest owl encounter was in Year Three of primary school. It was school photo day and as we lined up, a buzz of out-of-class excitement filled the air. Chattering and pointing up ahead signposted that something strange was afoot. After ten minutes of tiny steps forward, I saw what it was. Finally making it from the queueing corridor into the school hall, I saw a woman with a cracked tan leather handling glove and, clutching onto it with sharp talons, was a coffee-and-cream-coloured barn owl. Wow. What a thing to miss in the school announcements.

Its cavernous black eyes surveyed the room and, shining like copper under the artificial lights, it looked frightfully out of place above the wooden herringbone floor. Even this occasion did not spare us from the usual processing by teaching assistants: combing of messy hair, tightening of ties. When my turn came, I stepped forward and the owl – clearly accustomed to the camera – hopped onto my shoulder. Its soft feathers brushed against my cheek. Posing exactly as you would imagine the quintessential owl, like a yearbook photo from

Hogwarts, it stared directly down the camera. *Click* – it was over. Back to class.

Life moves quickly for an eight-year-old, and morning's news is evening's history. Neither me nor my brother said another word about it – goodness knows why not. When the photo arrived home four weeks later, my parents were amused but did not believe that it was real. A barn owl in school? You would expect it to pop up in conversation! Still surrounded by a bubble of disbelief, the photo rests proudly on the bookshelf to this day.

\* \* \*

Should one hear a badger call,
And then an ullot cry,
Make thy peace with God, good soul,
For thou shall shortly die.

Our ancestors felt it necessary to leave us this warning, dating back at least 200 years. "Ullot" is an archaic name for an owl which is similar to "howlet", a Scottish term meaning owl or owlet, so the rhyme is thought to be of Celtic origin. Like most creatures of the night, owls are perceived as ill omens, and simply hearing their sharp hoots and the tawny's wavering "tu-wit, tu-woo" could spell the worst. As late as the nineteenth century, an owl flying past the window of a sick person meant imminent death in Britain and yet, in parts of Northern England, seeing an owl was a sign of good luck. In times past, the barn owl could even act as a weatherman of sorts: its screech meant that cold, stormy weather was incoming and, if heard during foul weather, a change to bright skies would soon come.

# Singing Like Larks

A twelfth-century preacher known as Odo of Cheriton recorded his reasoning as to why owl species are largely consigned to dawn, dusk and darkness. He explained that an owl once stole a rose, the prize traditionally awarded for beauty, and was punished for his vanity by the other birds by allowing him to only venture out at night. Perhaps this was his sentence because, at night, the owl would no longer be able to see the beauty of the rose. This harassment persists today. In gardens with a few large trees, or land bordering woods and parks, a commotion erupts when a tawny owl is discovered in the harsh light of day. Smaller birds will mob the owl until it retreats back into its roosting hole.

In folk songs, owls have come to embody the darkness they inhabit, their calls forming the backdrop of eerie night-time walks. Clearly the owl represented an ill omen in parts of Scotland, just as it does in the Middle East, China, and Japan. The "weaver poet" Robert Tannahill (1774-1810) – so called because he was the son of a silk gauze weaver – used the howlet as such when he wrote one of Scotland's finest and most powerful night-visiting songs:

Are Ye Sleepin', Maggie?
O, mirk and rainy is the nicht,
There's no' a star in a' the cairey.
Lightning gleams across the sky.
And winds they blow wi' winter's fury.

*Chorus (repeated after each verse):*
O, are ye sleeping Maggie?
O, are ye sleeping Maggie?
Let me in, for loud the linn
Is roarin' ower the warlock's craigie.

# Be More Owl

Fearfu' saughs the boortree bank,
The rifted wood roars wild and dreary.
Loud the iron yet does clank,
And cries o' howlets mak' me eerie.

Abune ma breath, I daurnae speak,
For fear I rouse your wakeful daddy.
Cauld's the blast upon my cheek.
O rise, o rise my bonnie lassie.

Well, she's ope'd the door; she's let him in.
He's cuist aside his dreepin' plaidie.
Ye can blaw your worst, ye winds and rain,
Since, Maggie, noo I'm here aside ye.

O, noo that you're waukened, Maggie,
O, noo that you're waukened, Maggie,
What care I for howlet's cry,
For roarin' linn or warlock's craigie?

---

*Glossary:*

| SCOTS LANGUAGE | MEANING IN ENGLISH |
| --- | --- |
| *mirk* | dark |
| *cairey* | the heavens, sky |
| *warlock's craigie* | wizard's crag, enchanted rock |
| *fearfu' saughs* | frightening sighs |
| *boortree* | elder tree |
| *yett* | gate |
| *eerie* | afraid |
| *abune* | above |
| *daurnae* | dare not |
| *dreepin' plaidie* | dripping cloak |

# Singing Like Larks

Still sung today by The Tannahill Weavers, amongst other artists, it is usually backed by a fiddle and the rich-toned bouzouki in a lively arrangement. The bits of Scots language transform even the most southern of singers into a youngster traversing the wild glens and braes of the north through the howling night.

* * *

Obscure corners of the folk song tradition venerate the owl, paying no attention to their gloomy reputation as harbingers of bad luck. Surprisingly, this is most true in the early seventeenth century when owl superstition was rife; 'Of All the Birds' is undoubtedly one of the greatest homages paid to any bird, written by Thomas Ravenscroft (*c.* 1588-1635), an English musician and folk music collector.

### Of All the Birds

Of all the birds that ever I see,
The owl is the fairest in her degree.
For all the day long she sits in a tree
And when the night cometh away flies she.

Tu whit – Tu woo,
To whom drinks't thou? – Sir Knave, to thee.
My song is well sung, I'll make you a vow
That he is a knave that drinketh now.

Nose, nose, nose, nose,
And who gave thee thy jolly red nose?
Cinnamon and ginger, nutmeg and cloves:
And that gave me my jolly red nose.

In the second verse, the singer mimics the call of the tawny owl and rhymes with it. This goes a step further than other works included in this book: to not just sing about nature but to use its sounds. A musical collaboration between avian and human voices, in literal harmony with nature. No deeper honour can be bestowed upon the owl – imitation is the sincerest form of flattery, after all. This carol has indeed been "well sung" by Tim Hart and Maddy Prior, members of Steeleye Span, who lift their voices to exalt the fairest of all birds and the winter season.

The Druids, a folk band based in Co. Kildare, Ireland, deliver my favourite rendition of the song and their recording directed me towards the following tale of battle:

In spring 1807, a military campaign was undertaken in Egypt by the British. The southern Mediterranean city of Alexandria was occupied, and British advances were being halted by Turkish forces. As darkness fell the night before a disastrous foray, ending in the bloody battle of El Hammed, the tension was unbearable. The silence was drawn out while the men awaited almost certain death. Out of nowhere, one steely nerved soldier started singing 'Of All the Birds', and soon all the men joined in. For most of them, outnumbered twenty-to-one as day broke, that was to be their last evening. But what better way to spend it under such circumstances? For one shining moment in that sandscape, a leafy grove of Britain sprang up around them, cheering for the lusty human spirit, and the owl was saluted by all.

\* \* \*

# Singing Like Larks

Homage is still being paid to the owl today. Books come to mind like *The Secret Life of the Owl* by John Lewis-Stempel (Doubleday, 2017) and *Barn Owl: Encounters in the Wild* by Jim Crumley (Saraband, 2014). More broadly, acclaimed author Robert Macfarlane's *The Lost Words* (Hamish Hamilton, 2017) – illustrated by Jackie Morris – aims to conjure back the magic and mystery of the natural world for children through a series of poems.

Research has shown that primary school children today find it easier to name their favourite Pokémon character than a hare, deer or an oak tree. Revisions to recent editions of the *Oxford Junior Dictionary* have seen everyday natural words like "acorn", "bluebell" and "kingfisher" removed and replaced with techy words like "voicemail" and "broadband". Wild words are being forgotten just the same as folk songs. A new generation is emerging who are unable to tell a grebe from a goose, or a tawny from a barn owl. Macfarlane's *The Lost Words* project aims to rewild the language of children.

The follow-up *Spell Songs* project, released by Quercus Records in 2019, gathered together a range of artists to create a concept album about British wildlife. It includes 'Ghost Owl', a haunting song about the barn owl. It is sung by Kerry Andrew, composer and performer, and beautifully captures the "silence of silence", which characterises the owl's hunt – unseen, unheard. The line "Will you listen with owl ears" holds a valuable message for us all: speak less, listen more. Be more owl.

Projects like these are vitally important because we ultimately protect what we love. Nature-loving children grow into nature-loving adults, so wildness must be introduced from a young age – at grassroot level. In my Forest School sessions, yells of "Ew! Squish the bugs" in session one transform into "Let's build a bug hotel and make them a new home!" by session six. Those fortunate enough to grow up in a nature-loving household cannot expect others to automatically value what they have neither seen, heard nor experienced. We have to show them. Children need nature, and nature needs children.

\* \* \*

As well as Goddess Athena with her little owl, the ancient Greeks had another, rather wonderful belief. They believed that owls had a magical "inner light" which granted them their night vision. Our own inner light must be a deeply rooted love of wildlife. A love which allows us to see clearly. If you and I can shelter our inner lights from the world's extinguishing winds, then – like the wise old owl – we too shall glide seamlessly through the dark times.

# Jolly Old Hawk

## (*Accipitridae*)

*Once I had a grey hawk, a pretty grey hawk,*
*A sweet pretty bird of my own;*
*But she took a flight, she flew away quite*
*And nobody knows where she's gone.*

–'The Grey Hawk'

THE FIRST "HAWK" SONG that I encountered was not about hawks at all. Called 'Tramps and Hawkers', it describes the life of a hawker in Scotland, an antiquated name for a travelling salesman carrying inexpensive goods from town to town. These types of mobile street vendors were around for thousands of years in Britain, chanting and bantering with locals as they moved through the streets flogging their wares.

O, come a' ye' tramps and hawker lads an' gaitherers o' bla'[31]
That tramps the country round and round, come listen enn and all.
I'll tell to ye' a rovin' tale, o' sights that I ha' seen,
Far up intae the snowy north and south by Gretna Green.

# Jolly Old Hawk

"Hawk" is a versatile word – a lexical light refracting through a word prism. It refers to birds of prey with broad, rounded wings and long tails, but hawking is also the name for the feeding strategy of smaller birds who sally out from perches to catch insects on the wing. Rather unromantically, to hawk also onomatopoeically describes the noisy clearing of the throat.

The second song included here deals with an entirely different kind of hawking: the art of hunting game with a trained hawk. Although this rural pursuit (which is now largely called "falconry" – a term which covers all trained birds of prey) is closely tied to the land, the song in question came to me across the corrugated waters of East Anglia.

Every river, estuary and reed-whistling creek is a musical highway. A passage for songs to cut into the landscape, brought ashore as melodious cargo to be swapped and shared. They become part of that landscape; part of who we are. Songs journey from port to port in the seafaring mind, floating on the sailor's tide and coasting on the bargeman's breeze.

The Grey Hawk

Once I had a grey hawk, a pretty grey hawk,
A sweet pretty bird of my own;
But she took a flight, she flew away quite
And nobody knows where she's gone, my brave boys,
And nobody knows where she's gone.

So through the green forest I rambled away,
And across the green fields I did stray;
I hollered, I whooped, I played on my flute
Not my sweet pretty bird could I find, my brave boys,
Not my sweet pretty bird could I find.

# Singing Like Larks

So over the green hills I rambled away,
And along the green parks I did stray;
Lo, there I did spy my sweet pretty bird
And close by the side of a man she did lay,
She was close by the side of a man.

Now he that has got her is welcome to her
To do the best with her he can;
But whilst he has got, and I have her not
I will hawk with her now once and then, my brave boys,
I will hawk with her now once and then.

So happy's the man who has a good wife,
Far happier is he who has none.
But curs-ed is he who courteth his friend's
When he has a good wife of his own, my brave boys,
When he has a good wife of his own.

Originally this was a Restoration ballad (*c.* 1675) called 'Cupid's Trepan', beginning "Once did I love a bonny, bonny bird". A better-known version of the song is called 'My Bonny Bird' which, apart from the title, ignores any reference to birds at all. As A. L. Lloyd writes, 'The Grey Hawk' is "sung to a handsome variant of the 'Henry Martin' tune", one of the oldest and most beloved folk songs in existence. Of course, these lyrics are not really about hawks or hawking, but about women.

I first heard 'The Grey Hawk' from the singing of devoted bargeman Alfred William "Bob" Roberts (1907-1982). Unlike other traditional survivors, his version sticks close by the original tune printed over three centuries ago. He recorded it twice, first in 1960 for Peter Kennedy as part of an EFDSS EP called *Stormy Weather Boys!*, and again in August 1977 on his own LP released by Topic Records called *Songs from the Sailing Barges*. Bob remembered Vaughan Williams visiting his father – who ran the church choir – at their Dorset home to collect 'The Grey Hawk', amongst other songs. As he says at the end of the recording:

> *Vaughan Williams used to come an' copy songs down from my father. I can remember him coming to the house, a great big chap, we were sent out, my sister and I. My father used to play the fiddle and the squeezebox and the concertina and the violin, the piano, church organ – and he used to sing a lot.*

Bob Roberts lived a fascinating life. His course was set in 1906 – the year before he was born – in a shiplap, salt-panned corner of the Norfolk coast. The Everard family were well-known shipwrights working out of Fellowes Yard in Yarmouth, and the two apprenticed sons – Frederick and William – were each challenged to build a Thames sailing barge at a time when 2000 of these vessels traded along London's great river. Frederick built a ninety-one-foot barge called *Hibernia*. William built an almost identical vessel named *Cambria*. Both had gleaming white hulls and trim, rigged with oxblood sails and their names intricately carved on bow and stern.

These sibling barges worked as river and coastal cargo carriers, sailing across the Channel to Rotterdam, Antwerp, Dunkirk, Calais and Treport, delivering up to 170 tonnes of wheat, pitch, coal, pulp and other goods – enough to fill seventeen railway carriages. After a profitable working life of thirty-two years, *SB Hibernia* sadly sank in 1937 near Cromer in a frightful gale. *Cambria* had outlasted her (and has done by some margin).

Whilst these events were unfolding, a fifteen-year-old Bob Roberts had learnt to sail in Poole onboard various small fishing boats.[32] Then, one day, Bob was standing on the quay watching the barquentine *Waterwitch* unloading coal and got talking to the mate. He was invited to join the crew as cabin lad for a trip to Fowey. Bob accidentally failed to get off the ship before it left the town, and his parents subsequently received a telegram: "Ship didn't stop so am in Liverpool".

As one of his first jobs on the boat, the skipper asked Bob to preserve four-hundred eggs by smearing them in tallow. After about thirty eggs, he devised a plan. Melting the grease and dipping the eggs into the hot liquid would surely get rid of the job in record time. When the eggs came to be used months afterwards, the cook tried breaking them in a frying pan only to find a hard purple ball where the yolk should be. Bob laughed, recalling, "They'd been cooked about two months!"

Time soon did away with such youthful inexperience and, whilst learning his trade, progress was knocking down the door of western England. Schooners were increasingly being fitted with auxiliary engines but a fresh-faced Bob preferred working under sail so, in the 1920s, he relocated to the east coast where he moved cargo for Everard & Sons as mate and then skipper.

For the next thirty-five years Bob embarked upon many sailing adventures which took him all around the world. He worked on a total of eight barges, apart from a short stint as sub-editor of the *East Anglian Daily Press* in the late forties. It was not until 1949 that he moved to the quaint hamlet of Pin Mill, on the shipwrecked shores of the River Orwell in Suffolk, where he was offered the captaincy of the *Cambria*.

Coastal trade by sail was growing increasingly difficult as barges were being outcompeted by faster motor ships. Still, Bob revelled in his ability to harness the elements to reach his destination, carrying whatever to wherever it was wanted, be that timber to Southampton or cattle cake to Colchester. When Everard & Sons finally made the decision to sell their sailing barges in the early 1960s, Bob was given the opportunity to own the *Cambria* outright. He swiftly accepted and, with only an eighteen-year-old boy and Penny the dog as crew, they ran it successfully from 1966 onwards, delivering cargo around Essex and East Anglia.

A BBC documentary called *Look Stranger* (*c.* 1970) follows Bob for a day on a trip down the Orwell to his daughter's wedding in Pin Mill. Turning the *Cambria*'s spoked wooden wheel, he explains why he continued trading under sail while the world changed around him:

> *It takes so long to learn barging, sailing and seamanship that it seems silly to give it up. I mean, alright, give it up when you can't get your leg over the rail but otherwise I don't see any sense in giving up. If I wasn't barging, what should I do? I've been offered command of motor ships but all you do is stand there going boom boom boom from Christmas till Christmas watching her 'ead go up and down. What becomes of you?*

Continuing in between cries of "Ready about!", he sums up the attraction of a barging life:

> *One of the fascinations of this job, you know, of having a sailing barge is that we have to do exactly the same things as they did one hundred years ago. When Nelson brought ships in and out of here, he just had to do what we do, and we've*

*just got to do what he did. So you're carrying out a tradition*
*that's gone on for centuries and centuries... You don't work*
*with time, you work with the tides, with the sea, with the*
*wind — that's your life.*

Keenly aware of the changing winds, he continued, "How
much longer, I don't know. I'm getting older and so's the old
barge." As he spoke, a metal, slab-sided contraption of a ship
came chugging its way up the river on the left, taking Bob's
attention with it. "Let's get round 'er 'ead. If you lay alongside
a ship like that you'll catch something." A born raconteur, he
could talk for days about the Orwell, characters in the village,
how each channel got its name, and the history of local smuggling. With a mischievous twinkle in his eye, he says, "We
always like to say there's no smuggling now. But you've got to
tell 'em that ain't ya."

*Cambria* remained financially viable largely because her flat
bottom and shallow draught allowed her to enter water chan-
nels and make deliveries that other ships could not. The final
British commercial freight delivery made entirely under sail
was carried out by Bob and Dick in October 1970: 100 tonnes
of cattle cake from Tilbury Dock to Ipswich. *Cambria* had outlasted them all. Bob was the very last captain of a British commercial vessel operating under sail. For this feat, he was named
the "last of the sailormen".

Floating around the waterways of East Anglia allowed Bob
to collect a broad repertoire of songs and shanties from other
bargemen and those he met in the pubs. From the 1950s, he
was well-known for his authenticity and distinctive singing
style. His contracts to perform always specified that he would
appear "winds and tides permitting". With a squeeze of his

melodeon in The Butt & Oyster (the famous Pin Mill water-side inn, a pilgrimage for seafarers), the last of the sailormen lit up the air with a true sense of community and tradition. Dick Durham recalls that "everyone really joined in".

Bob died in 1982 aged seventy-four, having sold the *Cambria* to The Maritime Trust, where she laid in St Katherine's Dock for years. There she deteriorated: rotting timber and leaks in the ceiling. She was sold to the newly formed Cambria Trust in 1997 for one pound and a colossal £1.4 million restoration project began. Without their efforts, the tale I am about to tell would have been impossible.

One morning in July, clouds lurked in the distance. A dinghy picked a small group of us up at 7:00 a.m. sharp from Pin Mill hard and ferried us out into the river to where the *Cambria* was moored. We circled her completely before the skipper directed us to the ladder beside the fin-like leeboard on her flank. I stepped off the dinghy and climbed, holding on tight. My eyes passed over a thin line of yellow detailing on the side which I had never noticed in pictures. I swung my leg over the rail; I was on. With the third mate, nicknamed Shiner, we pulled together on the halyards to hoist the heavy sails. We were about to take part in the Pin Mill Barge Match, an annual race between Thames sailing barges travelling out past Shotley Point, where the Orwell meets the Stour, straddling Suffolk and Essex.

The wooden *Cambria* seemed vulnerable in the shadow of the unscalable container ships in Felixstowe Port. If something went wrong, there was only the anchor to save us. My mind raced trying to stow away the safety information being reeled off by the crew and I timed my movements to dodge the violent to and froing of the towering mainsail. "Switch on," I thought, "This is real." With fully rigged barges on all sides, nothing about the scene gave away its modern context. Sails and sailors all around, shouting instructions to each other. The experienced crew moved as one. By the time the weather finally rolled in, I was moving with them – winching, hauling, furling, sweating, and soaking up every minute of the bargeman's life, as well as my fair share of rain.

A moment of calm found me standing alone at the stern under a patchwork sky. With hot, rope-worn hands, I cast my eye upriver at returning boats and thought of Bob – how well he knew these waters, when he last stood where I did, and what he would think of the restored *Cambria*. After all, he did at one time express a wish to take her out to sea and burn her once she was no longer commercial. I hope a small part of him would be glad to see her still sailing and, with a steaming mug of tea from the galley topped up with rainwater, I sang 'The Grey Hawk' quietly to myself, drowned out by the gurgling wake.

\* \* \*

Now back to the hawk. 'The Grey Hawk' calls on a time as late as the nineteenth century when hawkers perceived these predatory birds as women in need of taming. Even today, to train a hawk is "to man" it. This is surprising because, although hawking was a popular sport until the 1950s and '60s, its peak was in the Medieval era amongst the European nobility when ladies were renowned for their falconry skills.

The earliest mentions of the sport hail from Saxon England in the ninth century and even the Bayeux Tapestry depicts scenes showing that hawks and falcons were owned by the

Anglo-Saxon kings of England at the time of the Norman Conquest. Such activity was limited to the upper echelons of society because birds of prey first had to be caught, before being trained rigorously to perch on the hand and hunt. Some were even bred specifically for the purpose.

*The Book of Saint Albans* was printed in 1486 and records the "Laws of Ownership". Under this set of regulations, only a king could keep a gyrfalcon – the largest falcon in the world, stocky and regal with striking white and dark colouring. A prince could own a peregrine falcon, a duke a rock falcon, an earl a tiercel peregrine falcon, a baron a bastarde hawk (an archaic name for a common buzzard), a knight a stalker, a squire a lanner, a lady a female merlin and a priest a female sparrowhawk. A hawk was a prized status symbol, giving rise to this hawk hierarchy, and to give one as a gift would have been a grand gesture indeed – but this is exactly what happens in the next song:

### Jolly Old Hawk
Jolly old hawk and his wings were grey;
Now let us sing.
Who's going to win the girl but me?
Jolly old hawk and his wings were grey
Sent to my love on the twelfth-most day.

Twelve old bears and they was a-roaring,
Eleven old mares and they was a-brawling,
Ten old cocks crawl out in the morning,
Nine old boars and they was a-quarrelling.

Jolly old hawk and his wings were grey
Sent to my love on the twelfth-most day.
Eight old bulls and they was a-blaring

Seven old calves and they ran before 'em
Six old cows and they was a-brawling,
Five for fif and a fairy.[33]

Jolly old hawk and his wings were grey
Sent to my love on the twelfth-most day.

A four-footed pig and a three-fistle cock,[34]
And two little birds and a jolly old hawk.

Jolly old hawk and his wings were grey;
Now let us sing.
Who's going to win the girl but me?

Another from The Watersons' enchanted *Frost and Fire* LP in 1965, the low harmonies and quick bouncing rhythm feel particularly ancient. It was originally collected by Cecil Sharp from William Chorley of Somerset in 1907, but The Traditional Ballad Index dates it to 1889. Little else is known.

Like 'The Twelve Days of Christmas', this is a cumulative song, sung as an Epiphany or Twelfth Night carol when the sun is at its feeblest and – as many once thought – demons roamed the land. A. L. Lloyd writes that at this time of year "certain ceremonies had to be observed and it was important to make no mistake in carrying them out, or penalties would be incurred". I wonder what the penalties would have been. Ceremonies and seasonal games were often accompanied by songs like 'Jolly Old Hawk' and the song itself could be a kind of memory game.

In Peter Kennedy's *Folk Songs of Britain and Ireland* (Cassell & Co, 1975), it is called 'The Jolly Gos-Hawk', and these exact words included above appear in Francis James Child's collection. Child was a nineteenth-century American folklorist who collected English and Scottish ballads, now known as the Child

Ballads. Number ninety-six is called 'The Gay Goshawk', a large bird with red eyes. It begins:

> O' well is me, my jolly goshawk,
> That ye can speak and flee,
> For ye can carry a love-letter
> To my true-love from me.
>
> O' how can I carry a letter to her,
> When her I do not know?
> I bear the lips to her never spake,
> And the eyes that her never saw.
>
> The thing of my love's face is white
> It's that of dove or maw;
> The thing of my love's face that's red
> Is like blood shed on snow.
>
> And when you come to the castle,
> Light on the bush of ash,
> And sit you there and sing our loves,
> As she comes from the mass.
>
> And when she goes into the house,
> Sit ye unto the whin;
> And sit you there and sing our loves,
> As she goes out and in.

The story continues for another thirty-two verses! The fair lady decides to meet the squire who has sent her the love letter from Scotland via the goshawk, and asks her father, mother, sisters and brothers that "If I should die in fair England, in Scotland bury me". They agree and she takes a sleeping potion from a "witch-wife". Her family thinks her dead and, when her body is carried to Scotland, the squire comes to lament her, opening the winding sheet:

"Set down, set down the corpse," he said,
"Till I look on the dead;
The last time that I saw her face,
She ruddy was and red;
But now, alas, and woe is me!
She's walowit [withered] like a weed."

The lady then wakes suddenly, laughing and asking for some of his bread for she has fasted for the last nine days. After asking her brothers to go home, she looks forward to her life with the squire and that is where it ends:

"I came not here to fair Scotland
to ly amang the dead;
But I came here to fair Scotland
To wear the gold so red."

Many variations exist and the original author is unknown. Heroines feigning death to win their lovers is a motif in ballads – I wonder if the squire still wanted to marry her afterwards! A bird as a messenger (like we saw with the robin), in this case the goshawk, is also a common occurrence in folklore but this seems strangely unrelated to the goshawk's usual portrayal as a symbol of strength in folklore. Upon researching the real-life use of hawks as messengers, I have been redirected at every turn to homing and carrier pigeons, unable to find a shred of evidence that goshawks (or any species of hawk) were ever used for such communicatory purposes. In fairness, the screeching goshawk speaks in this song, so I suppose it was not written as a historical document.

# Jolly Old Hawk

* * *

Smash and grab. That describes my most memorable encounter with a hawk. It was a balmy midsummer afternoon in the garden and the world was still. No hawk-like squeals. No alarm calls from smaller birds. No signs at all that a drama was about to unfold, until … feather explosion! A hapless wood pigeon was in the clutches of a female sparrowhawk. She noticed me and began to mantle her prey, arching her brown wings to guard her lunch and looking back at me over her long tail. Stamping. Plucking without mercy, revealing the brown bars on her breast and underwings which might as well have been the bars of a prison for this poor pigeon. No escape.

To have this life-and-death situation energetically swoop into a pyjama day felt like being thrown into a lion's enclosure. I saw first-hand that hawks get straight to the point. They are not good negotiators and are not out to make friends. That is why 'The Hawk and the Crow' is such a striking song, with all manner of woodland birds chatting together in harmony. However, to get there, we should start at the beginning.

William Thackeray printed a broadside in London *c.* 1689 containing a ballad called 'Woody Queristers' – a querister being a member of a church choir. A later broadside contains a line illustration representing a whole host of birds sitting in a woodland clearing around a log circle, with a version of the lyrics printed on the yellowed paper, looking as if it has been dabbed with a wet tea bag the night before a history project is due. This song does not mention a hawk, but does include the "cuckcow", sparrow, robin, lark, blackbird, nightingale and more. The seventeenth-century spelling and punctuation is its own:

# Singing Like Larks

**Woody Queristers** *(verses* **1-5***)*
When Birds could speak, and Women they,
Had neither good not ill to say?
The pretty Birds fill'd with pain,
Did to each other, thus Complain.

OH! says the Cuckcow, loud and stout,
I flye the Conntry round about:
While other Birds my young-ones feed
And I my self do stand in need.

Then says the Sparrow on her nest,
I lov'd a Lass but it was in jest
And ever since that self same thing,
I made a vow I neer would sing.

In comes the Robin and thus he said,
I lov'd once a well favoured maid:
Her beauty kindled such a spark
That on my breast I bear the mark.

Then said the Lark upon the grass,
I lov'd once a well favour'd Lass,
But she would not heare her true love sing
Though he had a voice would please a King.

The full version is a masterpiece, with each bird sharing their individual complaints. If I were to write a verse for the hawk, it would go like this:

Then says the Hawk, flying high,
I have no Lass but own the sky,
I've only twigs to build my home
And every day I hunt alone.

Over time, 'Woody Queristers' forked into multiple songs with a whole host of names like 'The Bird's Harmony', 'Leatherwinged Bat', 'The Bird's Courtship', 'Bird Song' and 'The Hawk and the Crow' – the song mentioned earlier.

Thought to have originated in Northern Ireland, at some point 'The Hawk and the Crow' moved across the pond to the USA and largely died out in the British Isles. In 1953, Peter Kennedy made a recording of this song from a tall, smartly dressed man named Liam O'Connor of Pomeroy, Co. Tyrone, noting that it was "a rare find", having only previously heard it in Cecil Sharp's collection from the Southern Appalachians made during World War I. Kennedy was delighted "to come across a version still being sung in its country of origin before its flight across the Atlantic". This is the version that Liam sang:

The Hawk and the Crow
Said the hawk unto the crow one day,
"Why do you in mourning stay?"
"I was once in love and I didn't prove fact
And ever since I wear the black."

*Chorus:*
Singing: Ri-the-diddle ri-the-diddle ri-the-diddley dum,
Singing: Ri-the-diddle ri-the-diddle ri-the-diddley dum,
[I was once in love and I didn't prove fact
And ever since I wear the black.][35]

And next there spoke the Willie Wagtail,
"I was once in love and I did prevail,
I was once in love and I did prevail
And ever since I wag my tail."

# Singing Like Larks

And next there spoke the little brown thrush
Who was sitting in yon holly bush,
"The way to court I've heard them say
Is to court all night and sleep the next day."

And last there spoke the Jeannie Wran,
"Do you know what I'd do if I was a man?
For fear that one would wriggle and go
I would wear two strings upon my bow."

These birds have clearly had troubles in love, so let us endeavour to minimise their complaints. During my research for this chapter, I was encouraged to learn from the BTO that damaged kestrel and sparrowhawk populations had bounced back by the mid-1970s after bans on harmful pesticides came into force, with this increase driven by improved nesting success. More recently, the conservation of hawks, falcons and eagles seems to be leading the way in wider bird conservation, with successful reintroductions of the red kite and the white-tailed eagle. Before being reintroduced, the white-tailed eagle had been absent from English shores for 240 years. We can take heart from these good news stories.

We have heard of jolly hawks, grey hawks and talking goshawks, yet we have heard no folk song that truly treats the fine-tuned hawk with the respect this bird deserves (*demands*, even). I would expect to find in the singing tradition more heroic regal epics and musical descriptions of battles where a hawk swoops in and saves the day. Alas, nothing. The closest I have come across is a version of a medieval English ballad called 'The Three Ravens', published in 1611, which places the hawk alongside a knight. Much more befitting for these valiant, stoical creatures!

The Three Ravens

There were three rauens[36] sat on a tree,
*Downe a downe, hay downe, hay downe,*
They were as blacke as they might be.
*With a downe, derrie, derrie, derrie, downe, downe.*[37]

The one of them said to his mate,
Where shall we our breakfast take?
Downe in yonder greene field,
There lies a Knight slain under his shield,

His hounds they lie downe at his feete,
So well they can their Master keepe,

His Hawkes they flie so eagerly,
There's no fowle dare him come nie

Downe there comes a fallow Doe,
As great with yong as she might goe,

She lift up his bloudy head,
And kist his wounds that were so red,

She got him up upon her backe,
And carried him to earthen lake,

She buried him before the prime,
She was dead her self ere euen-song time.

God send euery gentleman,
Such haukes, such hounds and such a Leman.[38, 39]

Shown here to be incredibly loyal, now it is our turn to return the favour. It seems that, only within the last few decades, we have woken up and begun to treat birdlife with the respect shown in the 'The Three Ravens'. To give just one example, from the 1840s, the development of efficient guns and their use in game preservation resulted in the indiscriminate killing of birds of prey until they were given legal protection in 1962. We lost our way slightly. But, today, charities such as the BTO support many young naturalists, all passionate about protecting our birds – hawks included – helping them to gain a ringing permit and add to our scientific quest for knowledge.

Simply hearing the plaintive, long 'peeeee-uu' note of a buzzard brightens my day immensely and that alone is surely worth protecting. Who knows, one day – like the slain knight in the song – a 'Hawke' might just save us too.

* * *

I do not usually expect to see a bird of prey, except for the bird-scattering marsh harriers at Rainham Marshes by the River Thames. I increase my chances of a sighting at home by regularly sitting in a reclining deck chair in the garden, swinging back and scanning the skies. The top of the nearby woodland's thick canopy remains visible over the staircase of roofs, and even more so when in leaf. This is my kind of hawking – hawk-watching. The only interruption is a visit from my dog, a fluffy pollen ball, licking my hand for attention, which is freely given.

Two buzzards often soar up there together, circling effortlessly on thermals like surfer dudes catching gnarly waves. Watching them resets my mind, unwinding with their spiralling. Whether it be a broad buzzard, a hovering "motorway hawk" (kestrel) or a sparrowhawk taking my garden fences for the walls of a colosseum, seeing one never gets old.

## *Jolly Old Hawk*

The buzzards live in the woodland alongside their smaller contemporaries, and after an afternoon of sky surfing, they settle down like me to listen to the woody queristers' evening performance. Sunset stage lights fade from orange to red, deeper than any kite. Songbirds sound high above the broad-leaf cathedral, their music carried weightlessly. The buzzards sit atop spire trunks pointing heavenwards, and dusk's notes echo till dawn.

Up flies the kite, down falls the lark O.

-'Padstow May Day Song', trad.

# Swan Song

## (*Cygnus*)

*Then she went her way homeward with one star awake,*
*As the swan in the evening moves over the lake.*

–'She Moved Through the Fair'

MUTE SWANS, the UK's only year-round resident swan species, are famously quiet creatures, except for mornings on the Norfolk Broads.

Kingfishers zip from staithe to staithe, flashing royal blue and princely gold whilst otters corkscrew and float past on their backs. A chilled mist from the night before sits deep in lowly hollows, not yet burnt off by the sun's fingers of light. And then a slight rippling, a gentle *plashing* sound is the daily alarm, changing the mood swiftly. The swans are patrolling.

Attending each moored-up hire boat like an angry press gang, they noisily bash and peck the white fibreglass hulls to rouse any sleepy holidaymakers who might have a few crumbs to spare. Raising their periscope heads over the side, staring eyes appear abruptly, somehow portraying their impatience without facial expression as they await their breakfast. That is the morning swan-call, and I have often been woken by it.

Swan-Call
Call of the swan and she in mist,
Call of the swan and she forlorn,
Call of the swan in early dawn,
Call of the swan the mere-face kist.[40]

\* \* \*

Until the late nineteenth century, farming had not changed in East Anglia for centuries. Almost every process was still reliant on manual or horse power of the four-legged kind. Agricultural labourers were skilled but often illiterate, so their unlettered minds brimmed instead with stories, poems and songs they had picked up over time.

On low wages and sometimes poor treatment, a farmworker was required to be a jack of all trades, and a master of them all too. Immense patience and understanding were required to mark out a field ready for ploughing, draw a straight furrow, broadcast the seed without leaving an unsown path, lay a hedge, cut hay with a scythe and thrash the corn with a flail – separating grains from their husks. It is under these demanding conditions that many of the songs in this book flourished, granting enjoyment and escapism to both singer and listener.

Bred and born next to Barton Broad in Norfolk, Harry Cox (*b.* 1885) was the seventh of thirteen children and worked the land all his life. To glance at in the pub, older men like Harry, fortified with decades of earthy practical experience under his flat cap, may not have appeared easily approachable. He held a pipe firmly between his teeth, his brown jacket fell from his broad shoulders, and his brow was furrowed from decades of physical work. His calloused hands were well acquainted with every intricacy of seed, scythe and plough.

One would be forgiven for thinking *How could I talk to him? Where would I start?* Entering into conversation with such a competent man of the soil holds an unsteadying mirror of judgement up to oneself, and yet Harry judged nobody. Throwing back his head, closing his brown eyes and releasing an old song from a deep core of organic purity, he was transformed.

Harry was interviewed in the front room of his cottage by Charles Parker and featured in a programme called *The Singer and the Song* alongside footage of herring fisherman Sam Larner, cut together to cover both land and sea. He wears a bobbly cable-knit sweater and skilfully lilts a "diddly-dum" tune, dangling in front of him a crudely carved wooden man attached to a metal gimlet. The man is jointed at the hips, knees and ankles so that, as Harry rhythmically bashes a thin plank beneath him with his fist, the little man dances a jig. "I call it 'Dancing Dom'. I made it meself," he said, when asked about the oddity by Charles.

"I've been knocking about on the land ever since I was able to do anything," he said plainly when asked about his upbringing. "My father didn't stick to land like I done, he went on the fishing." Chuckling with pride for his father, he continued with enthusiasm, "He done all sorts, he did! He wasn't tied to this lot [the land] like I was."

Preferring the outdoors to a schoolroom, Harry left formal education at twelve and a half at a time when each pupil had to pay "tuppence a week" which the family struggled to afford. But he was not done learning – far from it: "There's nothing I learnt there that I haven't learnt ten thousand times since I left. I was not one to read but I can read now. I learnt meself."

With the farm labourer's wage amounting to no more than ten shillings a week, the Cox family saw "more dinnertimes than dinners" but they still sung together, shouldering their burdens and counting their blessings daily. He picked up traditional songs from wherever and whomever he could, starting with his parents and grandfather, who were also talented singers. Occasionally he sang in the pubs for a few coins but more often alone in the fields to amuse himself whilst working.

As a young teenager, Harry went into stock feeding and was eager to learn, working seven days a week and using his rare days off to go "babbing" for eels on Barton Broad. At harvest time he reaped the barley and corn with a scythe and tied up the golden sheafs by hand, explaining, "You used to tie all day long. I used to take delight in it. I could tie that as quick as you like, so I was never afraid of nobody on that job. I done acres and acres."

Over the course of his life, he worked on various farms and sang in Sutton, Potter Heigham and Ludham pubs – including The White Horse in Neatishead, an annual Norfolk Broads stop for my family. This section of river is less travelled as most continue straight across Barton Broad and up the River Ant, rather than exploring the narrower, wilder dykes. It is kingfisher central, which is my mother's favourite bird.

Harry's father collected songs on his travels. He would pay a songster on land or sea to sing him a particular traditional tune over and over again until he had it memorised. Many of these were then passed on to Harry who, in his later years, had a mental archive of around 150 traditional folk songs. Harry's memory was astounding: "Up the present I ain't forgot anything yet," he said. This was his advice for remembering a song: "You have to get the tune first. If you get the tune, you'll get the song."

Spending his life next to the Norfolk Broads, Harry would have been surrounded by swans much of the time. It is no wonder that he was fond of 'Polly Vaughan', a tragic ballad. This song was collected by English composer E. J. Moeran who visited Harry in 1921, "discovering" him in a musical sense. Moeran arranged for him to be recorded for the first time in 1934 by Decca Records in London – the very first step in allowing us to enjoy his records today. The song concerns a young fowler and a mortal mix-up.

### Polly Vaughan

So come all you bold sportsmen that carry a gun,
I will have you go home by the light of the sun, –
For young Jimmy was a-fowling, was a-fowling alone,
When he shot his own true-love in the room of a swan.[41]

So the first he went to her and found it was she,
He was shaking and tremb-e-ling, his eyes scarce could see.
"So now you are dead, love, and your sorrows are o'er;
Fare thee well, my dear Polly, I shall see you no more."

Then home went young Jimmer with his dog and his gun
Saying: "Uncle, dear Uncle, have you heard what I've done?
Curs-ed be this old gunsmith that made me this gun,
For I've shot my own true-love in the room of a swan."

Then out came bold Uncle with his locks hanging grey –
Saying, "Jimmer, dear Jimmer, don't you run away.

Don't you leave your own count-e-rie 'til the trial comes on,
For you ne'er shall be hang-ed for the crime you have done."

Now the trial came on and pretty Polly appeared,
Saying, "Uncle, dear Uncle, let Jimmer go clear,
For my apron was wrapped round me when he took me for a
    swan,
And his poor heart lay bleeding for Polly his own."

The first time I heard Harry's recordings I was instantly struck by their honesty. No editing or digital enhancements; it is what it is. He even ends his moving performance of 'Polly Vaughan' by asking whoever was behind the microphone, "How's that?" His rumbling and beautifully unpolished Norfolk dialect emanates a rich candidness which does not impose on the listener, but simply lets the song shine. Even through my phone speaker, the room fairly shakes.

As one of the very last source singers, having learnt songs from the oral tradition, his vast repertoire and graceful under-standing of complex melody attracted the attention of song col-lectors like Peter Kennedy and the Lomax family in the 1950s and '60s who helped him record multiple unaccompanied solo records. It is safe to say that, without Harry Cox, the world of English folk music would be considerably diminished. He passed away in 1971 aged eighty-six, but his recordings, "rang-ing from rough bawdry to high balladry"[42], continue to inspire.

Renowned singer Shirley Collins met Harry in the 1950s at Cecil Sharp House in London, and her writing afterwards just about sums up this wonderful man:

*I was a teenager, so you might think that sitting listening to an elderly man singing unaccompanied songs wasn't the most thrilling event – and yet it was! A year or so later I listened to all of Peter Kennedy's recordings of Harry, and the more I heard, the more convinced I was of his absolute greatness, how melodious and graceful was his singing and how perfectly paced. But he was never dull. He could make you smile with 'The Maid of Australia' or move you with 'Polly Vaughan' and his 'Death of Nelson' is one of the most touchingly mournful songs I ever heard and does that great hero honour.*

*Harry convinced you with every song that he sang. He was modest in his demeanour in spite of all the praise that was so rightly heaped on him, but he learned and sung the songs, not to impress, but because he loved and valued them, and that was conveyed in his performances. Harry Cox had a rare grace and a genuine sweetness in both his person and his singing. I met him once and treasured it all my life.*[43]

\* \* \*

A rain shower comes on as Polly wanders back from her uncle's house. The sun is setting and, not wishing to get wet, she huddles beneath a green bush and wraps a white apron around herself for warmth and cover. Meanwhile, Polly's lover, young Jimmy, has been out hunting all day. With a rifle in hand and finger resting on the trigger, his eyes catch a glimpse of whiteness amongst the green leaves of the bush. Is it a swan's feathers? Maybe a light-coloured fawn's breast? In the falling darkness, he raises his gun and *fires* with a crack. The barrel smoke dissipates. Jimmy's stomach drops with horror and grief to find his lifeless love, white apron wrapped around her, dyeing puddles red with her blood.

# Swan Song

This story is an ancient one, permeating the folklore of many European countries and even forming the basis for Tchaikovsky's *Swan Lake* ballet. 'Polly Vaughan' in its ballad form is generally accepted to have originated in seventeenth-century Ireland, and perhaps even earlier in the oral tradition. Broadsides of this song began to appear in London between 1802 and 1819, and were then printed in York, Manchester, Cork, Dublin and even New York over the course of the nineteenth century. There are over a hundred versions to study and a namely trend emerges: versions hailing from the Emerald Isle tend to call the girl "Molly Bawn" – thought to be an anglicisation of the Gaelic "Mailí Bhán" which translates to "Fair Mary" – whilst versions from England call her "Polly Vaughan" (or "Vaughn").

The song itself also goes by many names, be it 'The Shooting of his Dear', 'The Fowler', 'Polly Vaughan', 'Molly Bawn', 'Molly Ban' or 'As Jimmie Went A-Hunting', illustrating just how popular and widespread the story used to be. It therefore puzzles folk historians and scholars as to why it does not appear in the Child Ballads, as James Francis Child would undoubtedly have been aware of it. Scholars' best guess is that Child's decision to exclude this song was coloured by comments made by Robert Jamieson, a contemporary ballad collector, in *Popular Ballads and Songs from tradition, manuscripts and scarce editions* (1806), after he heard it sung by a maidservant:

> *This is indeed a silly ditty, one of the very lowest descriptions of vulgar English ballads which are sung about the streets in country towns and sold four or five for a halfpenny.*

What Jamieson may have overlooked is that 'Polly Vaughan' seems to enshrine a relic of ancient European shapeshifting myths about women and children turning into waterbirds, either of their own accord or against their will by an envious person.[44] In early versions of the song she may have actually turned into a swan by way of some magical power, rather than being simply mistaken for swan-kind in a tragic moment of haste. If this is the case, then Polly could have in fact been a "swan maiden".

Swan maidens exist in the mythology of many countries, especially the Celtic nations, and are portrayed as serene women showered in beauty and draped in thin, unfathomably soft garments of swan feathers – usually depicted as wings – which allow them to fly. Swan maidens are gentle, exotically sensual and charmingly innocent. Whenever they appear in a folk tale, a version of the following narrative generally unfolds:

*A young, unmarried man – sometimes a hunter, other times a prince – spends the night in a clump of bushes on the edge of a pond, hoping to capture wild ducks. To his astonishment, at midnight he sees no ducks, but rather seven maidens clad in gleaming white feathered robes disrobing to bathe. He falls madly in love at first sight with the youngest of the swan maidens.*

*One evening, as they come to bathe again in a body of water, the young man creeps through the bushes to steal the youngest maiden's magic robe. As a golden sliver of sun sits on the horizon, the maidens gather their angelic garments and prepare to leave, but the youngest is unable to find hers. The older siblings wait for as long as they can but eventually leave her behind, calling out, "Meet your fate, whatever it may be." When the older sisters are gone, the hunter appears holding the feathered robe. She begs for its return so that she might fly away but the hunter, unwilling to lose her, refuses. Instead, he takes her home, hides the robe and marries her.*

# Swan Song

*The hunter attempts to domesticate the magical swan maiden. She is forced to remain human, estranged from her own world. She bears his children and lives a life weighted down by domestic drudgery. When the children grow older, they see their mother weeping and ask her why. She tells them, and they quest to find her feathered robe. They are successful and return it, and the weight is lifted from the maiden's shoulders as she slips it on, returning to her true fantastical self again. Her feet leave the ground, she glides towards the sky, and disappears the way she came. The children are left behind and grieve her loss, whilst the husband considers trying to find her, but the impossibility is clear, so he does not try.*

With ancient legends like this, it is not a stretch to suggest that 'Polly Vaughan' was once filled with magic from the same bottle. Poor Polly is likely a direct descendant of the mythological swan maidens but sadly she seems to have lost a large portion of her magical powers through the years. Her feathered gown has been taken from her and replaced with a white apron. And yet, a supernatural element remains in the final verse of Harry Cox's rendition, when Polly comes back as a ghostly apparition to ask for her love to go clear (be cleared of all charges).

In every version that I have ever heard, the outcome of young Jimmy's trial is left to the listener's imagination. Was he found guilty of murder? What about poaching? We will never know for sure. Whilst we cannot be certain of Jimmy's fate, I am satisfied that scholars and folklorists of the last century have connected this so-called "silly ditty" with its mystical roots, gifting Polly back her long-lost feathered gown and allowing her to fly as a swan maiden once again.

\* \* \*

# Singing Like Larks

The Irish magic does not end there. 'She Moved Through the Fair' is delicate, heart-breaking and an air of enchantment surrounds it, following the swan wherever it goes. It was first collected by a Co. Donegal poet called Padraic Colum (1881-1972) and musicologist Herbert Hughes (1882-1937).

## She Moved Through the Fair

My young love said to me, "My brothers won't mind,
And my parents won't slight you for your lack of kind."
Then she stepped away from me and this she did say:
"It will not be long, love, till our wedding day."

She stepped away from me and she moved through the fair,
And fondly I watched her go here and go there,
Then she went her way homeward with one star awake,
As the swan in the evening moves over the lake.

The people were saying no two were e'er wed
But one had a sorrow that never was said,
And I smiled as she passed with her goods and her gear,
And that was the last that I saw of my dear.

I dreamt it last night that my young love came in,
So softly she entered, her feet made no din;
She came close beside me, and this she did say,
"It will not be long, love, till our wedding day."

The tragedy in this song is far more understated than in 'Polly Vaughan', but no less cutting. Just as this young couple get the green light from her family to wed, she leaves the fair and dies. Like the young man, we don't know how she died. Returning to him at the end in a ghoulish dream (although in some versions it is not a dream, she actually returns as a spirit), she reassures him that they will soon be wed in the afterlife, assumedly when he passes on. I am not sure how comforting that would be.

I am far from the first to note that this song stands out from the crowd. It stays with you. Each lyric hangs like an icicle from branches reaching over the lake. Each word longs to be sung in a hall or church, where sad echoes can dance easily around the walls like voices of long-dead spirits who wandered home from the long-ago fair.

\* \* \*

Swan is not a very tasty meat, apparently. Stringy and a bit fishy is the verdict given by a portion of those who have tried one, whilst others liken it to duck. Since the twelfth century, the Seigneur of the Swans (a lesser used title for the British monarch) has had the right to claim ownership of all unmarked mute swans swimming in open waters, many of which have graced a royal banqueting table over the years. They are noble and delicate creatures, but also solitary and aggressively protective of their young, characteristics which make cob and pen the rightful king and queen of all waterbirds.

When mute swans were granted official royal status (the first mention of mute swans being a "royal bird" was in the late twelfth century), the right to keep them on the Thames was also granted to favoured landowners. Only two ancient institutions still exercise their rights: the Worshipful Company of Vintners (founded to control the selling of wine) and the Worshipful Company of Dyers (founded to control the sale of cloth) – both livery companies which were first bestowed their swan ownership rights sometime in the fifteenth or

sixteenth centuries. But how on earth do they fairly appor-
tion the Thames' mute swans among the three proprietors?
Therein lies the tradition.

"All Up!"

On the third week of July, this is the yearly cry of the
Swan Uppers when a family of swans and fluffy grey cygnets
are spotted. Teams from the Crown as well as the Dyers and
Vintners companies cast off in traditional wooden skiffs and
row the section of Thames from Sunbury Lock in West London
to Abingdon in Oxfordshire, where most of the river's swans
live. Winds flap the swan-adorned pennants and teams wear
different colours: scarlet for the Crown and, for the Dyers and
Vintners, blue and white. White swan feathers are pushed hor-
izontally into the peaks of caps.

This ceremonial occasion feels like a mini coronation each
year. Passing Windsor Castle, the rowers stand to attention with
oars raised and salute – "Her Majesty the Queen – Seigneur of
the Swans!"

Approaching a brood, three boats carefully form a tight
triangle around them. Hissing and puffy necks communicate
the swans' displeasure as the Uppers (as the crew are known)
jump into the shallows and lift them from the water, weighing,
measuring and sending them on their way. Half of each new
brood of cygnets automatically belong to the Crown, whilst the
remainder are shared equally between the two livery companies. In times past, the swans' beaks would have been nicked
into a particular shape or design to show which company they
"belonged to".

Today, Swan Upping has two primary goals: conservation
and education. School children get to see swans up close, and

the Uppers get a chance to check their health, especially the young vulnerable cygnets. The swans get a lightweight ring placed around their leg which is linked with the British Trust for Ornithology's (BTO) database. Scientists use this information to track breeding success and population change – both indicators of wider environmental factors such as water quality. This is truly a stellar example of a tradition emerging as a tool for wildlife conservation.

As with most traditions, like "Hunt the Wren", I expected there to be many traditional folk songs associated with Swan Upping. The closest thing is a song written by Ashley Hutchings, a founding member of three cornerstone folk rock bands: Fairport Convention, Steeleye Span and The Albion Band. It is called, appropriately, 'Swan Upping Song'. At first, I wondered whether it was traditional, but after getting in touch with Ashley, he told me that he wrote the lyrics himself and researched Swan Upping in detail as he did. It begins:

Me name is Harry Harris and I'll sing to you a song,
Concerning of a trip I made to mark the river's swans.
A dozen other mates and me set out one summer's morn,
And it was the toughest picnic boys that ever I was on.

*Chorus:*
We were jolly boys, we did no 'arm,
For four days on the roses we went a' Swan Upping like our
    fathers did before.

On July the twenty-first from the city we set off,
All gaily dressed in livery to row to Henley Lock.
In Vintners, Kings and Dyers cloaks of scarlet stripes and blue,
We went up the Thames in rowing boats, we were a merry crew.

# Singing Like Larks

In years to come, perhaps this song will achieve "traditional status" – a term which means something slightly different to everyone. After all, every song was written by someone, somewhere. It is time that adds the traditional magic when the details of its origin fall away.

\* \* \*

A tradition (musical or not) does not have to be shared by a country, a county or a team of Uppers – it can also be entirely personal. Most traditions are founded and renewed with our own friends and families. One of my family traditions is visiting the swans down at Hullbridge, a riverside town on the River Crouch in Essex.

Ferry Road slopes gently past eighteenth-century wooden-beamed cottages with tiny doors, down to the algae-green slipway. Sailing boats lean on their mud moorings and a rocky causeway reaches under the water and reappears on the quieter side of the river where park runners meet on Saturdays. That is where the mute swans usually are when we arrive, but they soon drift or waddle over (depending on the tide) at the sight of food.

Some snatch it out of my hands, scraping my fingers with their beaks, whilst their warier peers stay back. I try to be as fair as possible, accurately propelling a morsel to every swan and even providing for the rogue ducks caught up under the thick canopy of white wings. Bread never tastes better than when feeding it to swans, so I take a few bites for myself – granary, of course.

Squabbling gulls bombard the scene, catching crumbs on the wing. Overhead, honking wild geese fly in regimental V-shaped flight formations as if rallying for some distant waterfowl battle. A pair of mute swans glide down from this busy flightpath with necks straight as jousters' lances, looking far too stocky to fly. The air throbs with wing-power for the final descent and they water-ski on webbed feet for a moment to slow themselves. Landing successful. With a nonchalant wag of their tails, they swim on like nothing extraordinary just happened.

The whole experience brings me untold joy, come rain or shine. Flat fields, farms and only a few houses dotted across the water present a dramatic view of the evening sun, and halyards play windchime tunes against the masts. My parents first took me to Hullbridge and I hope to continue the pilgrimage always, reminded of swan songs which are still very much alive.

\* \* \*

As we approach the end of this final chapter, let us call upon Harry Cox once more, that lifelong champion of traditional folk music. "Keep 'em goin', these old songs," he encouraged. "If they do go, they're gone fo'ever – and no one will never know them no more." The same can be said of our bird species. Once they're gone, they're gone.

The fates of birds and folk songs are inextricably linked. If traditional songs die out, the birds nested within their lyrics will surely follow. But if folk songs flourish again – songs stemming from a time much more in tune with nature – then we may re-enter into a rich fellowship with our feathered friends. The choice is ours.

A folk song is a comfort, as is an interest in ornithology. Both are portable and can be taken with us wherever we go. All we ever need do is to sing an old song, or look skyward, to feel a connection with something far bigger than ourselves: all those who have carried a song through time and every birdsong ever sung, embroidered into an age-old tapestry of musical tradition and cycling seasons.

Birdwatching and folk singing possess that rare ability to focus the mind and melt away all cares for a few minutes. In those magical moments, nothing else matters. Harry knew this to be true and, backed by the chirping of birds, he cheerfully attests:

> *When I sing a song my mind is on it 'till I'm done. I don't let nothing else come into my mind. I let everything go. Keep your way clear so you know you're goin' right. Nothing don't trouble me.*

\* \* \*

The songs within these pages are just the beginning. There are so many more, waiting in the wings to be rediscovered.

# Afterword

## Rooks are Homeward Flying

A LOT HAS HAPPENED since I started writing *Singing Like Larks*. I went to London in the springtime to attend a gig by Ye Vagabonds, an Irish folk duo composed of brothers Diarmuid and Brían Mac Gloinn. They have added a cello to their usual mix of guitar, mandolin, rich Irish bouzouki and droning harmonium. In the intimate, darkened room, roaring waves could have been breaking right outside the stage door as the bow across the metal strings mimicked the distant calling of gulls.

Diarmuid explained that more and more Irish folk musicians are introducing atmospheric soundscapes and wild ambiances into both traditional and original arrangements, bringing birdsong and other natural sounds into the heart of the music, as well as the lyrics. Our ancient musical relationship with birds is clearly far from over.

# Singing Like Larks

Towards the end of 2021, I noticed on the Copper Family's social media page that they were due to perform a carol concert in December. I could not believe the venue: the local cricket club, a two-minute walk from my house across playing fields. What turn of fate led the Copper Family, who very rarely gig outside of their native Sussex, to venture north of the Thames to perform in deepest Essex? It just so happens that they are old friends with a local musician and event organiser and play for him at the cricket club every other year. What are the odds?

I secured three tickets straight away – one each for my dad, my brother and myself – which were popped through the letterbox just a few days later. I held onto them for a while, because the Coronavirus pandemic spiked, pushing the gig further and further back, whilst the Coppers remained resolute in their festive intentions, assuring ticket holders that "carols WILL BE SUNG" despite the approach of spring. Then storms came, damaging the cricket club's roof and forcing a venue change for the gig to the old fire station, turned arts centre, in the town.

A date was decided for March and about thirty people attended, all sitting facing two big red fire station doors at 8 p.m. sharp. About ten of the modern-day Copper Family sat and stood around a folding trestle table, covered with family songbooks and cups of good ale from the makeshift bar in the corner. All attention was focused on the now elder statesman and woman of the group, John and Jill (Bob Copper's son and daughter), as John twanged his tuning fork against the edge of the table, searching for the right pitch, before dryly announcing that "the table's in tune".

Since fate had brought us this far, something within me just knew which song they would sing first and – after a false start and a shared laugh – the family burst into familiar harmony:

One May morning early I chanced for to roam,
And strolled through the field by the side of the grove.
It was there I did hear the harmless birds sing,
And you never heard so sweet, and you never heard so sweet,
You never heard so sweet as the birds in the spring.

I was home – figuratively and quite literally, under a mile from my front door.

John turned from his songbook in his brown tweed jacket at the end of the gig to see my brother and I approaching and remarked in his thick Sussex accent, "Well that seemed to go alright, didn't it?" It really did. 'The Birds in the Spring' first welcomed me into the world of traditional folk music, and, without it, this book may never have come to fruition. I had travelled full circle in two years from that life-changing drive home from Malham Tarn in March 2020 when the rustic voices of the Coppers lit up the BBC 2 *Folk Show*, to this moment – listening in person to their sons, daughters and grandchildren singing the very same lyrics, and I singing along with them late into the evening.

Day is done, no use denying,
Sun is sinking, light is dying.
Rooks from fields are homeward flying,
Day draws to its close.[45]

# A selection of other bird-related folk songs

'The Banks of the Mossem'
'A Week Before Easter'
'When Spring Comes In'
'The Game Cock'
'The Contented Countryman'
'The Mallard'
'The Pleasant Month of May'
'Young Hunting'
'The Bird Upon the Tree'
'With Kitty I'll Go'
'Carrion Crow'
'The Oak and the Ash'
'Rosebuds in June'
'The Mountain Streams Where the Moorcocks Crow'
'May Morning Dew'
'The Little Ball of Yarn'
'Twas on One April Morning'
'My Singing Bird'
'The Royal Blackbird'
'The Rose of England'
'Twa Corbies'
'Curragh of Kildare'
'Brigg Fair'
'The Boys of Mullaghbawn'
'Three Drunken Maidens'
'Peggy Gordon'
'The Blackest Crow'
'Lament to the Moon'

# Endnotes

1. *A Song for Every Season*, Bob Copper (Heinemann, 1971, pg. 1).
2. *Journal of the Folk Song Society,* Vol. 1, No. 1 (1899).
3. *As I Walked Out* (verse 3), trad, from the Copper family's repertoire.
4. Trad, printed in *A brief Description of Pleasures* in 1656.
5. 'The Factory Girl', part of Makem's vast repertoire.
6. From the Copper Family repertoire.
7. 'The Holly and the Ivy' (verse 1), trad folk carol.
8. Hootenanny: a Scots term for a party. US term for an informal gathering with folk music.
9. https://sounds.bl.uk/World-and-traditional-music/Keith-Summers-Collection/025M-C1002X0087XX-0200V0
10. Jacobs, J. (1892) 'English Fairy Tales', G. P. Putnam's Sons, New York, London.
11. Trad. rhyme, origin unknown.
12. 'To the Cuckoo', William Wordsworth
13. https://www.bbc.co.uk/news/av/science-environment-36837641
14. Verse 4
15. Roud 1506
16. Roud 3000
17. https://www.youtube.com/watch?v=kjWn-RmKGSE
18. 'The Night Visiting Song' https://www.youtube.com/watch?v=W-MGvQ2v-ZRM
19. *The Blackbird and the Thrush*, Irish trad.
20. Source singer: someone who learnt songs from the oral tradition.
21. 'Windy Old Weather'
22. 'Singing the Fishing' (1960) is one of eight radio documentaries ("radio ballads") written by Ewan MacColl, orchestrated by Peggy Seeger and produced by Charles Parker. It features Sam Larner and Ronnie Balls of Yarmouth and is described as "A tribute to the fishing communities of East Anglia and the Moray Firth".
23. "Home fishing" means that the fisherman would return the same day.
24. After the final line in each verse, repeat the part in brackets three times before finishing the line again.
25. 'St Kevin and the Blackbird', Seamus Heaney (1996).

26. Quotes from *Songs & Southern Breezes: Country Folk & Country Ways* (William Heinemann, 1973), with permission from the Copper Family.
27. Somerset rhyme, but variants exist throughout Britain.
28. Roud 23614. Bob Copper collected a very similar version called *If I were back 'ome in 'Ampshire.*
29. Scots: "gloaming" means twilight, dusk.
30. Translated from Polish.
31. "Bla'" means scraps of wood collected from bushes and fences and carried in sacks.
32. As an adult, Bob's own fishing boat was named *Stormy Petrel.*
33. "fif and a fairy" = fieldfare.
34. "fistle cock" = "thistle cock" which is likely a corn bunting or thrush.
35. The chorus lines in brackets change to the last two lines of each verse.
36. In printed text of the time, *u* and *v* were often used interchangeably.
37. Lines in italics repeated in each verse.
38. 'Leman' = 'sweetheart' as seen in 'Sweet Lemeney'.
39. Other versions, like that of the 1970s Norwegian folk rock band *Folque*, place the hawk high up in the clouds or away hunting game and therefore unaware of the goings on below – their arrangement is called 'Ravnene'. The ravens eat their meal in peace.
40. Scottish trad., verse two.
41. "in the room of" is dialect for "in the place of".
42. *Oxford Dictionary of National Biography* (ODNB)
43. East Anglian Traditional Music Trust: http://www.eatmt.org.uk/harry-cox/
44. See also 'The Six Swans', a German fairy tale collected by the Brothers Grimm in 1812, the Greek myth 'Leda and the Swan', the Irish legend 'The Children of Lir' in which the children are transformed into swans for 900 years by an envious stepmother and 'The Wooing of Étaín', an Irish eighth- or ninth-century folk tale.
45. Penned by Bob Copper, included by permission of, and with thanks to, the Copper Family.

# Acknowledgements

This is my first book, and I am enormously thankful to Sara Hunt, founder of Saraband – a wonderful independent publisher – for taking a chance on me. Sara has helped me through the publication process and immediately shared in my vision for this book. Additionally, thank you to my editor, Rosie McCaffrey, for your kind, constructive and enthusiastic comments on the unpublished manuscript – I hope you can recognise, through changes made, a part of yourself in the text.

My family have tirelessly supported (and, at times, graciously put up with) my birdy musical obsession, listening to countless songs and proofreading almost everything I have ever written. Two little words don't repay such a huge debt but, all the same, thank you.

Sincerest thanks also to The Copper Family of Rottingdean – past and present – for their constant inspiration, and specifically to Jon Dudley and Jill Copper for checking over sections of the text. Your comments were a great encouragement and I hope that the contents of this book convey just how much the family's songs, and southern breezes, have guided me.

I would also like to doff my cap to Alex Long, Essex Wildlife Trust ranger at Fingringhoe Wick, for proofreading the opening two chapters and leading me to my very first turtle dove sighting. And, last but by no means least, my heartfelt thanks go to Stephen Moss for his beautiful foreword and for championing this book since it was a tiny seed of an idea. Your words and advice instilled a belief within me that getting this work published might actually be possible. For that especially, I am grateful.

Singing Like Larks would not exist without the inspiring folks mentioned here, as well as the coastal and country characters peppered throughout. Perhaps only songbirds could aptly sing their praises.

**Andrew Millham** is an emerging nature writer whose work has been published in national publications including *BBC Wildlife, Coast* and *The Countryman*. He graduated with a first-class honours degree in environmental science, has received a Field Studies Council Young Darwin Scholarship and – after completing his training with Essex Wildlife Trust – is now a Forest School leader, teaching outdoor skills to primary school children. He is also a keen folk singer.

*For a list of links to where you can find, hear or see a video of most of the songs in this book, scan the QR code below.*